REALISM

This book addresses one of the fundamental topics in philosophy: the relation between appearance and reality. John W. Yolton draws on a rich combination of historical and contemporary material, ranging from the early modern period to present-day debates, to examine this central philosophical preoccupation, which he presents in terms of distinctions between phenomena and causes, causes and meaning, and persons and man. He explores in detail how Locke, Berkeley and Hume talk of appearances and their relation to reality, and offers illuminating connections and comparisons with the work of contemporary philosophers such as Paul Churchland and John McDowell. He concludes by offering his own proposal for a "realism of appearance," which incorporates elements of both Humean and Kantian thinking. His important study will be of interest to a wide range of readers in the history of philosophy, the history of ideas, and contemporary philosophy of mind, epistemology and metaphysics.

JOHN W. YOLTON is Professor Emeritus at the Department of Philosophy, Rutgers University. He is the author of many publications on John Locke and on the history of philosophy more generally, most recently *Perception and Reality: A History from Descartes to Kant* (Cornell University Press, 1996).

REALISM AND APPEARANCES

An essay in ontology

JOHN W. YOLTON

Professor Emeritus, Rutgers University

PUBLISHED BY THE PRESS SYNDICATE OF THE UNIVERSITY OF CAMBRIDGE
The Pitt Building, Trumpington Street, Cambridge, United Kingdom

CAMBRIDGE UNIVERSITY PRESS
The Edinburgh Building, Cambridge CB2 2RU, UK http://www.cup.cam.ac.uk
40 West 20th Street, New York, NY 10011-4211, USA http://www.cup.org
10 Stamford Road, Oakleigh, Melbourne 3166, Australia
Ruiz de Alarcón 13, 28014 Madrid, Spain

First published 2000

Printed in the United Kingdom at the University Press, Cambridge

Typeface Monotype Baskerville 11/12½ pt.   *System* QuarkXPress™   [SE]

A catalogue record for this book is available from the British Library

Library of Congress cataloguing in publication data

Yolton, John W.
Realism and appearances: an essay in ontology / John W. Yolton
p.   cm.
Includes bibliographical references and index.
ISBN 0 521 77227 3 (hb). – ISBN 0 521 77660 0 (pbk.)
1. Ontology.   2. Appearance (Philosophy)   3. Reality.   I. Title.
BD311.Y65   2000
111–dc21   99-34668 CIP

ISBN 0 521 77227 3 hardback
ISBN 0 521 77660 0 paperback

For Jean

We shall have hereafter to enquire into the nature of appearance, but for the present we may keep a fast hold on this, the appearances exist. This is absolutely certain, and to deny it is nonsense. And what exists must belong to reality.

F. H. Bradley, *Appearance and Reality: A Metaphysical Essay*, pp. 131–2

'Tis certain, that almost all mankind, and even philosophers themselves, for the greatest part of their lives, take their perceptions to be their only objects, and suppose, that the very being, which is intimately present to the mind, is the real body or material existence.

Hume, *A Treatise of Human Nature*, p. 206

Contents

Preface

In a series of books from 1983 to 1996, I have examined various themes in seventeenth- and eighteenth-century philosophical writings. In *Perceptual Acquaintance from Descartes to Reid* (University of Minnesota Press and Blackwell, 1984), the themes primarily related to perception and our knowledge of external objects. The pervasive notion of "presence to the mind," with its accompanying principle of "no thing can be or act where it is not," raised puzzles about how the mental can relate to the physical. The implication often was that there can be no cognition at a distance. The consequences of these notions and principles seemed to be that we cannot know objects directly or in themselves. Those who grappled with these consequences, both well-known and lesser-known writers, struggled to find a way of breaking out of what some later commentators described as the "veil of ideas." *Perceptual Acquaintance* explored various interpretations of the nature of ideas and of the relation, causal or epistemic, between the perceiver and the world.

Thinking Matter: Materialism in Eighteenth-Century Britain (University of Minnesota Press and Blackwell, 1983) examined Locke's fascinating suggestion that God could have made thought a property of organized matter, presumably the brain, instead of making it a property of immaterial substance. The possibility that matter could be active, that it could be the substance or subject of both extension and thought, threatened many accepted views about the immateriality of the soul, to say nothing of traditional morality. That possibility also reinforced the newly emerging concept of matter, matter as active force and power instead of the older passive corpuscular structure waiting to be activated by God or other spirits. This newer concept had implications for perception theory, the nature of the objects we know, and the relation between ideas and objects.

There were three theories about this relation: occasionalism, pre-established harmony and physical influence. I gave a detailed account of the presence of these theories in eighteenth-century thought in France in my *Locke and French Materialism* (Clarendon Press, 1991). The reactions to Locke's suggestion and to his stress upon sensations as one of the sources of ideas and knowledge included attacks by many defenders of traditional doctrines, as well as adoptions by some of the French *philosophes*. While any materialism resulting from thinking matter in Locke's formulation, and as found in eighteenth-century Britain, had some significant differences from the materialism of Diderot, Holbach and others in France, the way in which we as perceivers acquire information about the environment of physical objects was a common theme in Britain and France, sparked by the suggestion of thinking matter.

I traced most of these theories and issues in a more systematic and developmental fashion in *Perception and Reality: A History from Descartes to Kant* (Cornell University Press, 1996). The central focus of that study was on ideas, representations and realism, and the ways in which these three terms might go together. I suggested that, in the writings of the main figures (Descartes, Arnauld, Malebranche, Locke, Berkeley, Hume and Kant), we can follow a gradual emergence of a clear translation or transformation of the old ontological language of presence to the mind into an epistemic presence. Arnauld spearheaded this transformation, but bits and pieces of it are found in Locke's coexisting qualities, and Berkeley's and Hume's talk of ideas as the very things themselves. Kant gives us a complex, detailed articulation of what we might call an epistemic realism.

Kant's combination of transcendental idealism and empirical realism recognizes the dual role played by the perceiver and objects in the production of perceived appearances (representations, ideas). The "objects" in this process are not the objects we know, the known objects that result from the mind's interaction with stimuli from the precognitive environment. Those "objects" work on us by means of "affection," a technical term Kant employed to suggest how the cognitive process begins. Known objects inhabit the world of appearances.

In this new study, I address the question: "Can we have a realism of appearances?" I limit my examination to Locke, Berkeley and Hume (with some brief reference to Kant's notion of agent causality). I begin with a look at the tendency found in some recent writings to deny or ignore the appearances. A few other recent writers are discussed who raise again the topic of the relation between mentality and physicality. In discussing a few current writings on philosophy of mind and cognitive psychology, I do so from the point of view of what I know about seventeenth- and eighteenth-century philosophy: an historian of philosophy looking at some contemporary writings. Doing so helps me to illuminate and perhaps make more relevant the views and worries of earlier philosophers. There are some similarities and some significant differences (differences which are important for an appreciation of the nature of ideas as appearances in Locke, Berkeley and Hume) between those periods and some of the contemporary issues in our time. The rejection, downgrading or ignoring of the appearances by some contemporary writers, their easy application of phenomenological, psychological and cognitive terms to the brain and neural events, hold a lesson for us. We should admire the efforts made by Descartes, Arnauld, Locke, Berkeley, Hume and Kant to find ways to explain the relation between physical and cognitive events, to face the difficult task of formulating a concept of object based on experience, and to do so without succumbing to either subjective idealism or reductive materialism.

Except for a few paragraphs in chapter 4, which are taken from my *Locke Dictionary*, none of this material has been published before. An earlier version of chapter 2 was presented to a seminar in the Center for Filosofi at Odense University in Denmark. I would like to thank my hosts there, Professor David Favrholdt and Dr. Jørn Schøsler, for providing me a forum for some of my ideas and for making my visit to Odense with my wife so enjoyable and intellectually stimulating.

   I have dedicated this book to my wife, my partner in scholarship, my in-house editor and skilled proof-reader. Her efforts over the years have consistently improved my prose, catching obscure and difficult sentences and passages in need of clarification. Her bibliographical skills are apparent in all my books.

Piscataway, New Jersey

Introduction

The distinction between appearance and reality is as old as the history of philosophy. Efforts to save the appearances have taken various forms, usually sparked by attempts to devalue appearance in favor of reality or "the really real." Sometimes, in our history, saving the appearances has been motivated by claims to reduce appearance to reality, or even, it seems, to deny appearances altogether. A less drastic tactic offers to *explain* the appearances in terms of items in reality. To say the appearances are not real does not, of course, get rid of them; their status (however characterized) must be reckoned with. Trying to ignore them is difficult; phenomena and qualia are tenacious. It is even more difficult to attempt to reduce them to items in reality, to their causes. It is salutary to keep in mind a remark by Bradley: "Whatever is rejected as appearance, is, for that very reason, no mere nonentity."[1]

The locution "nothing but" is frequently used when philosophers discuss appearances. The appearances are said to be "nothing but" particles or corpuscles, for example, or structured brain events. Even Thomas Hobbes, who recognized and honored the appearances, employed the "nothing but" locution frequently. That locution did not mean he denied the appearances or reduced them to matter and motion. Hobbes's materialism is at best an explanatory one, not an ontological one. He was very firm: there *are* appearances (phantasms) *and* reality (matter and motion). Our contemporary materialists are not so clear about what they are affirming or denying. Often, they seem to me to confuse two claims: (a) all phenomena, all seemings or appearings, can be *explained* in terms of or by reference to, e.g., brain events, and (b) there *are* only brain events (and other physical events in the environment). The recent vogue for talking about supervenience may be an attempt to have

---

[1] F. H. Bradley, *Appearance and Reality: A Metaphysical Essay* (London: G. Allen and Unwin, 1893), p. 135.

it both ways, somehow to combine (a) and (b). Perhaps the appeals to supervenience are a genuine recognition that phenomena, qualia and mental events are also real, also exist.

To follow claim (a) rigidly may eliminate the need for any causal explanation of appearances, qualia or awareness. Whether supervenience is a causal relation, I am unclear. Most often, it seems to be treated as an explanatory relation: awareness or consciousness arises from, or emerges out of, a specific organization and structure of brain processes. But whatever the relation is, to talk of supervenience would seem to lead to the recognition that what supervenes, what arises from, differs in some ways from that from which it has emerged, or what it supervenes on: the supervenee and the supervened would seem to differ, at least numerically. With perceptual qualia or phenomenal properties, the difference cannot just be numerical. There is a kind difference between seen color or heard sound and the physical and neural events that precede our experience of color or sound. Similarly, being aware of tables, computers, or coffee differs in kind from the physical and neural processes that correlate with such awareness.

Appearances take various forms and they are referred to with different words: "phenomena" and (in recent uses) "qualia" are the two most used besides "appearance."[2] Hume's formulation of the ordinary view about our knowledge of the external world is in terms of "perceptions," a term for what appears to perceivers. The ordinary view, Hume claims, does not distinguish perceptions from objects: "The very sensations [sense-perceptions] which enter by the eye or ear are with them the true objects."[3] In another passage, Hume uses the term "image": "The very

---

[2] The term "appearance" can be ambiguous; it has been used in a variety of ways in philosophy and literature. Basically, it refers to what contrasts with a reality not directly available to experience and observation. For some account of the appearance–reality distinction in the history of philosophy, see my entry under that title in the *Dictionary of the History of Ideas*. The entry for "appearance" in *The Encyclopedia of Philosophy* is also helpful. The specific use of "appearance" in my study will become clear in what follows. The "qualia" in recent discussions occurs in debates over various forms of materialism. Joseph Levine traces its use to C. I. Lewis: "it refers to qualities such as color patches, tastes, and sounds of phenomenal individuals. In this sense the term means what Berkeley meant by sensible qualities or later philosophers meant by 'sensa' or 'sense-data.' Since the demise of sense-data theories, the term qualia has come to refer to the qualitative, or phenomenal, character of conscious, sensory states, so mental states, not phenomenal individuals, are the subjects of predication. Another expression for this aspect of mental life is the 'raw feel' of experience, or 'what it is like' to have certain sensory experiences. Qualia are part of the phenomenon of the subjectivity of consciousness, and they pose one of the most difficult problems for a materialist solution to the MIND–BODY problem." (*The Encyclopedia of Philosophy*, Supplement, entry for "Qualia.")

[3] *A Treatise of Human Nature*, ed. L. A. Selby-Bigge, 2nd edn, revised by P. H. Nidditch (Oxford: Clarendon Press, 1978), p. 202.

image, which is present to the senses, is with us the real body."[4] The passage from Hume reproduced at the head of this study strikingly runs perceptions and objects together, not just for ordinary people, but for philosophers too, most of the time. We frequently speak of the appearances of objects to perceivers, we describe the way objects appear to us, but Hume is offering a radical proposal: perceptions *are* the objects. From "the appearance of objects to us," Hume (and Berkeley too) moves to "appearances are the objects themselves." The appearances have surely been saved with this move, they have been turned into reality! But at least for Hume, the perceptions we have do not exhaust reality. Hume still strives to retain a material world independent of perceivers. He has both appearances and reality, perceptions and objects, two aspects of the real.

My exploration in the distinction between appearance and reality revolves around a series of contrasts or distinctions which can be found throughout the history of philosophy but is particularly invasive in the seventeenth and eighteenth centuries. Most of these distinctions have also flourished in the twentieth century, especially in some recent analyses in philosophy of mind and cognitive psychology. Their presence in modern (of the seventeenth and eighteenth centuries) as well as in twentieth-century philosophy highlights many similarities in the work of philosophers in those periods. Contemporary philosophers and historians of modern philosophy are not always aware (at least, not fully aware) of the issues, concepts and questions they share. The invidious division between "philosophy" and "mere history" has done much to keep the two approaches apart. There is a tendency among the former to show only a superficial interest in the historical traditions behind them; they sometimes show an attitude of condescension towards those traditions. Both so-called historians of philosophy and "pure" philosophers can learn from each other. Contemporary work in cognitive psychology and philosophy of mind can illuminate the theories and doctrines of seventeenth- and eighteenth-century writers. A good, detailed and accurate knowledge and understanding of the latter can benefit and provide balance and some humility for the former. It is useful to remind recent writers that some of their problems and solutions are not new. Value is added to our study of modern philosophy when we discover the anticipations of recent, more sophisticated analyses. The history of philosophy need not be isolated in time, and recent contemporary philosophers should not be ahistorical.

---

[4] *Ibid.*, p. 205.

    The distinctions or tensions (Kant used some of them in his paralogism) that I have in mind are the following:

(1) Appearance and reality
(2) Phenomena and their causes
(3) Action and body motions
(4) Person and man
(5) Two languages – phenomenal and neural

    The relation between appearance and reality, when dealing with perception and our knowledge of the external world, is often said to be causal. A question can be raised: "are items in reality the sole cause of phenomena, of sense qualia?" Conceivably, reality need not require perceivers or cognizers, but can we conceive of qualia without perceivers? Some recent writers seem to replace the perceiver with functioning biological bodies, at least with the brain and neural networks. The perceiver gets reduced to an organized body, mind becomes the brain, body motions become actions, man becomes the person. These are steps taken for a variety of reasons, from a conviction that science, especially neurological science, can explain all, to a distrust of perceiver-dependent qualia, or to a disdain of the mental, the immaterial, the nonphysical.

    If we look down the above list of distinctions (perhaps we should call them categories), we can see that the left-hand members of the first four identify categories that usually go with perceivers, cognizers and actors, those to whom the phenomenal qualia present themselves. The fifth on the list refers to the language describing what is presented or what appears to perceivers, in contrast to the language for talking about the right-hand members. The first four right-hand items need not involve any reference to perceivers or cognizers or actors. The odd feature is that those philosophers who try to ignore, get along without, or just by-pass any reference to the left-hand items are themselves perceivers and cognizers trying to use the language of reality or neural events only, i.e., non-perceiver related processes. They are, as it were, situated in one domain, that of the left-hand members, but looking through or past that domain into items, often theoretic items, in the domain of the right-hand members. To have a greater interest in neural events than in our experiences of colors, sounds, shapes caused by (at least correlated with) those events, is a perfectly proper undertaking, but to fail to notice that their access to those neural events is mediated by perceived qualia (and some theory) is less understandable and rather odd.

    Philosophers of perception are faced with somewhat the same situation as those who, from the vantage point of the left-hand domain, construct theories of reality constituted only by members of the right-hand domains. That is, philosophers of perception have tried to look through appearances to the underlying reality. They have not always ignored the appearances, however. The problem for perception has been raised as a question: "what information about reality (e.g., physical objects, matter) can we find in our perceptions, in the appearances to sense?" The history of perception theory is filled with attempts to bridge the two domains: causal theories, representative theories. Related issues sometimes engulf perception theory: mind–body relation (e.g., parallelism, pre-established harmony), substance and quality metaphysic. What I want to do in this study is to nibble at the edges, hover around the periphery of some of these issues, rather than make a full-scale assault on the main problems. A full discussion of those problems in the seventeenth and eighteenth centuries can be found in several of my previous books, *Perceptual Acquaintance* and *Perception and Reality*. In this study, I concentrate my attention on issues directly related to perception: a defense of sense qualia and appearances, and their ontological status; the person as actor or perceiver; the nature of the object of perception; the role of mental contents; the causal or significatory relation between perceptions and objects. While my attention is clearly focused on these topics in seventeenth- and eighteenth-century writers, I also have an interest in the issues themselves, in their persistence in different times and places, including our own time. I hope I can clarify some particular aspects of the views advanced by Locke, Berkeley and Hume on perception and reality, while at the same time show their relevance to contemporary concerns.

I first turn my attention to the way in which the five-fold distinctions are at work in some recent writings on perception, action and knowledge. Chapter 1 examines two recent writers, one of whom (Paul Churchland, *The Engine of Reason, the Seat of the Soul*, 1995) tries to ignore or deny phenomenal qualities or redefines them as properties of the brain; the other (Clyde Hardin, *Color for Philosophers*, 1988) who, while defending the status of qualia as experienced phenomena, sometimes employs language which seems to overlook such phenomena. Churchland's analysis of neural networks in the brain, and his ambivalence on how mental events are related to brain events, raise issues familiar to students of modern philosophy who remember Locke's suggestion of thinking matter. The question then and now is: if thought is a property of the brain, does that turn thought into neural events? Churchland seems antipathetic to the notion of mental events, so thinking matter for him tends to become just matter, active but still matter. The title of his book mentions reason and the soul, but there is little of either in his account. The mind gets lost in Churchland's neural networks. One way in which it gets lost is in his failure to recognize the phenomena of awareness, of sensory qualities, of the appearances to the investigator of neural events and theory. The appearances get absorbed by brain events, the very language of mind gets applied to neural events, thereby seemingly replacing cognitive events such as understanding, recognizing, feeling and perceiving with neural analogs. This linguistic inversion or capture is just the reverse of the language used by seventeenth- and eighteenth-century philosophers when writing about cognitive events: they employed physical language and metaphors for descriptions of mental events. Unlike Churchland, these writers did not intend to say psychological events were physical events. Churchland seems to say or at least imply that neural events are psychological events. This difference is of interest in itself; it may also give us a better appreciation of the writings of seventeenth- and eighteenth-century philosophers. So in discussing Churchland (and Hardin to some extent), I am still addressing the issues of the earlier centuries. Perhaps my treatment may be useful for those philosophers who may not want to immerse themselves in those prior figures but who have some awareness of some of the similarities between those writers and our contemporary philosophers and psychologists.

Chapter 2 focuses on that important issue in seventeenth- and eighteenth-century writings, the relation between physical processes in the environment and the brain *and* processes of thinking, perceiving, seeing, etc. In particular, the question of our knowledge of so-called external objects was fundamental in much of those writings. I have made some suggestions about a gradual recognition from Descartes to Kant of two kinds or two different relations here: a physical causal relation between physical objects and brain events, and another, perhaps cognitive or semantic relation between brain events and mind (or the perceiver). One recent philosopher, Frank Jackson, writing on the subject of mental causation, strongly rejects the notion of two different relations. His argument is another by-pass of mental processes, this time it is believing or belief that turns out on Jackson's account be a brain state. The causation of action for Jackson seems to be only physical; ordinary beliefs and intentions do not seem to play any role. There are other recent writers (E. J. Lowe, Howard Robinson, Grant Gillet, David Chalmers) who have made some suggestions about the second kind of relation. I select just a few of these writings for some brief discussion, again as a way of showing similarities between old and new, but also as a means of showing the importance of a cognitive, semantic, meaning or informational relation between brain and mind or the perceiver. A side issue concerns the move from talk of the being of objects *in* the mind to the *being known* of objects. The language of presence to the mind has a way of appearing even in very recent writings. I do not track this issue in this study, but since it is relevant to the question of how physicality relates to mentality, I have a few words about it in chapter 1.

The first two chapters call attention to the way in which appearances (especially qualitative appearances) tend to get overlooked in the hands of some of our contemporary materialists, those appearances that we might characterize as cognitive appearances or what appears to a perceiver. And chapter 2 explores the relation between physical events and perceptual appearances. Chapter 3 focuses attention on the third and fourth items on my list, actions and body motion *and* the person and man, as these are developed by Locke and Kant. E. J. Lowe's interpretation of Locke comes in for some comment. The suggestion I make in that chapter is that actions as opposed to motions, and person as opposed to man, provide a way in which we can conceive and assign to phenomena (appearances, qualia) an ontological status similar to that which Locke and Kant assigned to actions and persons. This chapter is in a way a bridge between the first two and the final four chapters.

Chapters 4 and 5 explore the commitment of Locke and Berkeley to an ontology of appearance, of empirical objects; chapter 4 provides an inventory of Locke's use of the phrase "the things themselves," and some discussion of word-signs and idea-signs; and chapter 5 provides an inventory of Berkeley's extended use of the term "notion" along with his redefinition of "ideas" as the things themselves. I show in that chapter, by an examination of the occurrences of the terms "notion" and "notions" in Berkeley's writings, that he uses those terms in a variety of ways, not (as is usually thought) only for referring to spirits, God and relations. My conclusion there is that it is not "notions" that is the technical and radical term in Berkeley's thought, but the redefinition of the term "idea." My methodology in these chapters is to present the reader with the data, using a detailed inventory of key terms, rather than summarizing those data. I think it important to present the relevant passages in this way and then draw my conclusions. In a way, the inventories speak for themselves.

Chapter 6 examines Hume's use of the term "appearance" and the related term "perceptions," showing the range of items that are said to appear to the mind. While detailing the many passages in his *Treatise* and the two *Enquiries* that have physical objects appearing to us, I call attention to some striking similarities of language between Descartes's notion of objective reality and Hume's talk of the *being* of objects in the mind. I end that chapter by arguing that Hume's world is not limited to what appears to us, even though his requirements for meaning restrict our ideas and our vocabulary to perceptions. Chapter 7 then proceeds to analyze the many passages in the *Treatise* and the *Enquiry concerning Human Understanding* which speak of the world of external objects, a world of real causes and powers. There is a vigorous on-going debate on this topic, highlighted by Kenneth Winkler's article, "The New Hume" (*The Philosophical Review*, 1991). I do not want to consider the pros and cons of this debate presented by those who have been engaged in this discussion, although I do have some comments on Winkler's article. I try to let Hume speak for himself. The Conclusion attempts to sketch an outline of a realism of appearances. Some attention is paid to John McDowell's Kantian analysis in his *Mind and World*.

I

Mind, matter and sense qualia

Whether or not mental states turn out to be physical states of the brain is a matter of whether or not cognitive neuroscience eventually succeeds in discovering systematic neural analogs for all of the intrinsic and causal properties of mental states.

Paul Churchland, *The Engine of Reason, the Seat of the Soul* (1995), p. 206

Whatever explanation of cognition will in the end prove satisfactory, we can at least suppose that only one kind of existence – the real kind – will be involved. Ockham did not share the faith of many today that the mind is wholly physical. But if the mind must be explained in terms of the nonphysical, at least it need not be explained in terms of the nonreal.

Robert Pasnau, *Theories of Cognition in the Later Middle Ages* (1997), p. 85

Traditionally, especially within the period of Modern Philosophy (e.g., from Descartes to Kant), when philosophers turned their attention to perception and our knowledge of the external world, a standard set of issues, problems, principles and concepts were invoked, assumed and occasionally modified. A recent statement of the representative theory of perception characterized that theory as holding to two claims: mental operations of the mind arise "from causal impingement by the world" and the mind has "mental states and events which represent the world."[1]

[1] Grant Gillet, *Representation, Meaning and Thought* (Oxford: Clarendon Press, 1992). He calls this the empiricist representational theory. Another recent more detailed account of this theory (also referred to as "the causal theory" or "indirect realist theory") is given by Robert Oakes, who says that "awareness of (the surface of) external objects – of those objects that are before our sense-organs – can take place only by virtue of awareness of entities which constitute their effects upon our sensory apparatus. Entities of this latter sort are not, of course, before our sense-organs, but, to the contrary, are interior to consciousness. Moreover, it is clear that these phenomenal 'qualia' or private objects of awareness are such that their *esse* just consists in our awareness of them" ("Representational Sensing: What's the Problem?", in *New Representationalisms: Essays in the Philosophy of Perception*, ed. Edmond Wright (Aldershot: Arebury, 1993), p. 70). The term "qualia," as used by Oakes and others, replaces the older "idea." In treating qualia as private objects internal to consciousness, Oakes is able to state the representative theory in its usual, traditional form.

Analyses of the representative relation varied and questions were raised about the causal relation. Some writers became uneasy with the notion that mental contents (ideas) could be caused by physical (brain) events. That uneasiness was not due entirely to the acceptance of an ontology in which physical events are assigned to one kind of category or substance, and mental events to another kind of category or substance. There are passages in Descartes, Glanvill, Cudworth and, later, Kant that indicate a two-fold relation between perceiver and the world: a physical causal relation from objects to brain, and a significatory or semantic relation between brain and mind.[2]

It was generally recognized that the way the world appears to us, the world *as known*, differs qualitatively from the world itself, the world *that is known*. The usual vocabulary for talking about, even for describing, the world as known was the language of ideas. Hobbes used the term "appearance" rather than "idea." Kant talked of "representations," but he also employed the term "phenomena" when referring to the world as known. "Appearance" and "phenomena" avoid the idealistic and mentalistic implication of "idea," which, it is thought, makes the world a set of mental ideas; but a case can be made for saying that the term "idea" did not have idealistic implications for most of the writers (even Berkeley) who employed it.[3] Descartes's use of the term "idea" was a modification of scholastic "intelligible species"; his use was reinforced by other French writers such as Malebranche and Arnauld, and in Britain by Locke's heavy employment of the term. The vocabulary of ideas was also a way of adhering to two common principles: "no cognition at a distance" and "what is known must be present to the mind."

Those principles played an influential role in the history of perception theory, even appearing in our own time. Malebranche used those principles to defend his account of ideas as special entities present to the mind. Physical objects, he argued, cannot be present to the immaterial, nonphysical mind. Arnauld lectured Malebranche on the concept of

Footnote 1 (*cont.*)
  I have argued that the term "idea" in the writings of Locke does not always fit this internalist interpretation. With Berkeley, "idea" comes out of the closet of the mind, as it does also for Hume. My use of the term "qualia" in this study tries to make it refer to external qualities, qualities that are sensory appearances to perceivers.
[2] I have presented and analyzed this second interactive relation in *Perception and Reality: A History from Descartes to Kant* (Ithaca: Cornell University Press, 1996), ch. 8 (1996). See also *Perceptual Acquaintance From Descartes to Reid* (Minneapolis: University of Minnesota Press and Oxford: Blackwell, 1984), ch. 11. See also chapter 2 below.   [3] See my *Perception and Reality*, ch. 6.

"presence," insisting that "present to the mind" could only be taken as a cognitive presence: to be present to or with the mind just means is known or perceived by the mind (or the person). Arnauld got rid of Malebranche's special idea entities, opening the way he believed to a realism, possibly even a direct realism. Direct realism does not rule out ideational contents in the perceptual process. Other philosophers, including some very recent ones, seem to think direct realism requires objects themselves to be present with the mind, apparently failing to appreciate Arnauld's lesson about cognitive presence. These later writers also seem to equivocate on the nature of presence, literal or metaphorical.[4] Arnauld's analysis is more forthright in distinguishing spatial presence from cognitive presence. That distinction was not always explicit in subsequent writers, but it does resurface in Berkeley's careful explication of "existence in the mind" and it was, I believe, instrumental in the development of what I have called "the epistemic shift" in perception theory from Descartes to Kant.[5] That shift, the change from the language of ontology (the being of the object in the mind) to the epistemic language of being known, is of fundamental importance for understanding modern philosophy.

The concept of mind also underwent some changes in the modern period. From designating (along with "soul") an immaterial substance with ideas as modes or properties of a substance and as possessing various mental faculties and operations, the substance nature of mind gradually gave way to functional features. In some writers, mind was

[4] I called attention in *Perception and Reality* (ch. 4) to some articles in *Mind* as recently as 1986 where the notion of presence to or with the mind is employed in an ambiguous way in arguments against direct realism. Even more recently, Ruth Garrett Millikan uses that notion in her Patrick Romanell Lecture on Philosophical Naturalism, "How We Make Our Ideas Clear: Empiricist Epistemology for Empirical Concepts" (printed in the *Proceedings and Addresses of the American Philosophical Association*, November 1998). Professor Milllikan wants to locate the mind and its contents "among the natural objects" (p. 67). She says, sounding like Malebranche, that "knowing about other natural objects is not constituted by the presence of those objects directly within or before the conscious mind." On the same page, she goes on to say "The original or most immediate objects of reference are not before the mind but in the natural world." She remarks rather emphatically that "Just as with external objects, we cannot take properties of external objects to be in or directly before the mind. That would not be a 'natural' place for the properties of external objects to be!" She chastizes Russell for assuming, as she interprets him, that knowledge by acquaintance requires the object to be in the mind: "I hope it is fair to say that few today will accept Russell's picture of what it is to know what one is thinking about. If one thinking about an external object, knowing what one is thinking of cannot be having the object of thought within or before the conscious mind" (p. 69). I think we can say that the notion of presence to the mind is one of the most curious and persistent notions in the history of philosophy.
[5] See *Perception and Reality*, Conclusion, pp. 215–22.

more or less replaced by the operations themselves, such as thinking, willing, believing, sensing, imagining, etc. The language of mind was often borrowed from the language of physical objects. There was not a ready-to-hand psychological vocabulary. Most writers were aware that physical object language does not apply literally to mind and its operations; some even warned of the dangers of using that language. Metaphors and analogies of mirrors, dark closets, impressions, force and vivacity were used in efforts to describe and characterize mentality.

All writers in the early modern period were aware of the underlying physiology, even neurophysiology, of mental operations: mentality is supported by physicality. Some rather detailed physiologies were described and theorized about; some authors even postulated very specific correspondences between mental processes and states *and* neurophysiological areas and activity.[6] But neural and mental operations, brain and mind, were hardly ever identified as the same; they were not merged into one in the accounts given by those writers. Materialism was frequently charged, as against Hobbes or Spinoza; but those who leveled these charges ignored (as do many writers today) Hobbes's very explicit distinction between appearance and reality, and few understood that Spinoza's one substance possessed both extension (physical) and thought (mental) properties. If the first of these properties made Spinoza's substance material, the second should make it immaterial, but that subtlety was lost on most critics. It was just that combination of physical and mental properties in one substance that led to Locke's being seen as a materialist, or at least as lending support for materialism. Locke had of course made the suggestion that thought could be made a property of certain organized matter (the brain), without thereby reducing thought to extension.[7] Other writers after Locke, e.g., Priestley, Toland and Diderot followed this path, but only after developing a concept of matter that was largely force and power, not corpuscular (hard, impenetrable, inactive) particles.[8] These writers softened the distinction between thought and extension, but those properties were still different sorts of properties and activities associated with brain matter.

[6] I discuss some of the eighteenth-century physiologists who explored these specific correlations in *Locke and French Materialism* (Oxford: Clarendon Press, 1991).
[7] For a discussion of Locke's suggestion, and the controversy it aroused, see my *Thinking Matter: Materialism in Eighteenth-Century Britain* (Minneapolis: University of Minnesota Press and Oxford: Blackwell, 1983).
[8] Diderot and many medical researchers in the eighteenth century talk of muscle and nervous tissue as having the property of irritability. Hence, their concept of matter was directed towards the living body. Such matter had activity as part of its nature.

I

Priestley liked to say that he immaterialized matter. If we find that characterization too rooted in the traditional language of two substances, material and immaterial, we can still recognize the changed concept of matter from dead, inactive to active, live matter. When today, Paul Churchland[9] asserts that "Matter itself is neither intrinsically alive nor intrinsically dead," and then explains that "certain complex organizations of matter will be alive if they function in certain ways, and dead if they fail thus to function," we can ask "what are the ways in which matter can function so as to meet the criterion of alive?" (p. 190). Noticing that the terms "organization" and "complex" in this statement remind us of the very similar language used by Locke in his suggestion of thinking matter (*Essay* 4.3.6), we can ask "does that alive matter have thought as one of its properties or functions?" In one passage, Churchland comes close to the view suggested by Locke and adopted by Priestley, that the brain has both physical and mental states (p. 203), but there he is characterizing Searle's account, so he is probably not speaking in his own voice. He does not use the term "thought," so we cannot answer the question put in those terms. "Consciousness" is the term he uses. It is not clear just what the status of consciousness is in his account, he seems somewhat ambivalent about it. On the one hand, he suggests that it does not have any unique metaphysical status (p. 189): just as biological life has "turned out to be an intricate but purely physical phenomenon", consciousness might have a similar "fate" (p. 191). On the other hand, there are passages in which he says consciousness "is at least a real and an important mental phenomenon," a phenomenon "that neuroscience must acknowledge as a prime target of its explanatory enterprise" (p. 213). The suggestion here seems to be that a neuroscientific *explanation* of consciousness would somehow affect its metaphysical status, or even eliminate any such status. "Metaphysical" and "nonphysical" designate features that Churchland does not like (cf. p. 196). A neuroscientific explanation of the *phenomenon* of consciousness (an "explanatory reduction") is a substitute for a *metaphysical* or *ontological* reduction of the phenomenon to neural functions and structures (p. 223).[10]

Churchland does not give up on the stronger, more decisive reduction.

---

[9] *The Engine of Reason, the Seat of the Soul: A Philosophical Journey into the Brain* (Cambridge, Mass.: MIT Press, 1995).

[10] For an extensive defence of phenomenal consciousness, see Charles P. Siewert's *The Significance of Consciousness* (Princeton: Princeton University Press, 1998).

At least, in a number of places he employs the language of a status-reduction (a phrase I use to avoid the metaphysical vocabulary he does not like). He locates the contents of consciousness (he does not, I think, say what the contents are) in specific areas of the brain (p. 224). The status question will apparently be resolved in favor of brain states if neuroscientists succeed in discovering "systematic neural analogs for all of the intrinsic and causal properties of mental states" (p. 206). Neural analogs will dissolve that of which they are analogs! Perhaps he does not want to go that far, since later he refers to future neural imaging techniques that may enable us to "watch real-time neural activity as the conscious subject is engaged in any number of perceptual, cognitive, deliberative, or motor activities" (p. 300). The perceptual, cognitive, deliberative and motor activities of the subject will be *correlated* with, not reduced to, neural activity.

The same ambivalence can be found in other passages where he uses the language of full status-reduction. For example, the taste of a peach (he writes "subjective taste") "just *is* the activation pattern across the four types of tongue receptors, as re-represented downstream in one's taste cortex" (p. 23). Later, he softens this claim: it is *possible* that "the taste sensation of a peach is identical with a four-element activation vector in the gustatory pathways" (p. 193; cf. p. 205). Elsewhere, in speaking of finding a home for sensory qualia, he says the "problem is to find a plausible home for them within a purely physicalistic framework" (p. 250), but two pages later he returns to correlation, not eliminative, talk (p. 252). However, on p. 208 he is quite explicit about the program he has in mind: "If science is to achieve a systematic reduction of mental phenomena to neural phenomena, the demands it must meet are stiff indeed. Ideally, it must reconstruct in neurodynamical terms all of the mental phenomena antecedently known to us." If this reconstruction can be done, "it should also teach us some things about the behavior of mental phenomena that we did not already know, things that arise from hidden peculiarities of the neural substrate." That program sounds like a full status-reduction, despite the reference to mental *phenomena* (and also to "thermal phenomena" in the same passage). In these paragraphs Churchland also speaks of the explanatory domains of science, so there may still be some uncertainty about what sort of reduction he intends.

Churchland sometimes writes, in less reductive terms, of mental phenomena as just the systematic *expression* of "suitably organized physical phenomena" (p. 211); various phenomena are said to be *associated with* specific brain events (p. 212), or he writes of cognitive phenomena that might be *realized in* "some physical or electronic network" (p. 212). Such phenomena are also said to *arise* "naturally in a recurrent [neural] network" (p. 219); recurrent networks are also said to *produce* "typical conscious phenomena" (p. 221). I would think that examples of typical conscious phenomena would be my thinking about Churchland's effective examples and analogies, my seeing the blue jacket of his fascinating book, my hearing the logs in my fireplace snapping as they burn, my recalling some passage about thinking matter in Locke's *Essay*. Churchland says he wants to develop a theory "of cognitive activity and conscious intelligence that is genuinely adequate to the phenomena before us" (p. 235), but the theory he finds adequate is one that builds on the complex and specific neuroscience presented in his book. From his point of view, with his knowledge of the latest technologies, research and theories in neuroscience, conscious phenomena such as those on my list are made intelligible and understandable "on purely physicalist assumptions" (p. 206). An understanding of the neural correlates of particular conscious and cognitive experiences makes those experiences intelligible to him.

Precisely what an understanding of neural networks will yield about conscious phenomena, what it is about mentality that is rendered intelligible by such an understanding, is not at all clear from Churchland's account. It would seem too strong to say he denies consciousness and mental phenomena, because he does speak of them and says they are correlates of neural events which they express. His inclination seems to be to shy away from anything that might be nonphysical, but it is just those nonphysical states and events that he wants to explain and perhaps identify with neural networks. At best, I would say his language is ambiguous; perhaps he is ambivalent about the mental.

There are some similar but less pronounced ambiguities (but not, I think, ambivalence or confusions) over the status of cognitive or mental phenomena and the qualia of appearance in another recent important study, C. L. Hardin's *Color for Philosophers*.[11] But Hardin is emphatic about protecting phenomenal descriptions: "we need not and cannot forego" such descriptions (p. 111). He also says that sensory phenomenology "must be taken very seriously" (p. 134). He is not concerned in this work with the description or analysis of phenomena, or of the sensory domain. His concern and contribution is an account of the neural bases of the "perceived qualitative similarities and differences" in our color

---

[11] *Color for Philosophers: Unweaving the Rainbow*, expanded edn. (Indianapolis: Hackett, 1988).

experiences (p. 131; cf. p. 132). Those qualitative features are (as Churchland also says) an *expression* of "the neural coding," conscious phenomena are *represented* at the neural level, they are *embodied* in neural structures (p. 112). The *ground* of the resemblances between certain colors "must come from outside the phenomenal domain and yet it must bear an intrinsic relationship to experienced color" (p. 132). Hardin also speaks of a phenomenal-neural mapping (p. 137). An understanding of our sensory phenomenal experiences can be had from the details of the neural coding of those experiences, the coding may even *account for* our experiences (p. 135). I am not sure I understand what it would account for – just the existence of sensory experience, e.g., of visual experiences, of seen color? That there is a biological and neurological substrate to conscious experiences cannot be denied. Precisely how that substrate "determines" the visual experiences is more difficult to discover. Does the rich knowledge of detailed, specific correspondences that Hardin describes yield an understanding of how a phenomenal domain comes into being? We can say that, without the biological substrate, there will be no phenomenal domain, but does that fact indicate a relation of identity? The program of accounting for, of explaining, the phenomenal in terms of the details of the neural structure certainly is important.

I guess that the details of neural coding give us more information about phenomenal experience than just specific correlations, but none of those details would *describe* the experience. Description would have to be done in phenomenal and psychological language, not in neural language. Keeping the two languages and the two domains separate although closely linked is what I take Hardin to be doing, but his interest in that work is mainly in the neural domain. He uses a nice dictum, "render unto matter, what is matter's." I urge a corresponding dictum, "render unto phenomena what is phenomena's" or, "render unto experience what is experience's." However, there are a few places where his language seems to go against this important distinction. For example, he writes: "qualitative similarities and differences among sensory states amount, in the final analysis, to similarities and differences in sensory coding" (p. 133). The "sensory coding" refers, I think, to neural coding. If so, he seems to say the sensory *amounts to* the neural. How strong is "amounts to"? On p. 137, he says we could *identify* "color perceptions with a biological substrate." The term "identify" is rather strong. Has he not violated his insistence on not denying the phenomenal (perceptual) domain?

Hardin characterizes the account of the neural bases of color experiences as "materialism," assuring us that materialism is "capable of dealing with the qualitative character of sensory experience" (p. 134).[12] At the same time, he occasionally makes a claim stronger than just "understanding" or "accounting for" or "dealing with": he speaks of "transposing questions about the phenomenal colors into questions about neural processes" (p. 114) and he suggests, as we just saw, that we could *identify* "color perceptions with a biological substrate" (p. 137).

II

I have claimed that when Locke suggested that God could have added the property of thought to certain organized matter (i.e., the brain), he did not mean thought would then cease to be thought.[13] Under this possibility, the brain would have two different kinds of properties, contradictory properties according to many of his contemporaries. Similarly, I suggest that Priestley's or Diderot's active matter of the brain would still preserve the difference between physical and mental activity: a dualism of properties and of different kinds of activity.[14] These writers resisted the temptation to identify the one property or action with the other. If we consider them to be materialists (as many of their contemporaries did), we should recognize that it was not a status-reductive materialism. Nor were the systems of Hobbes and Spinoza materialisms of this sort.

The more recent talk by our contemporaries of sense qualia and conscious phenomena seems at first glance to be calling attention to the differences between these and neural phenomena. It would appear that they too recognize a difference of kind between these phenomena, between my thinking about what these writers say, my seeing red roses in my garden, my hearing the sounds of clocks, bells, birds and whatever complex neural activities that are the (necessary) condition for my conscious mental states. But both Churchland and Hardin (the former much more than the latter) tend to blur the differences; both make some forthright claims of identity between phenomenal and neural. Whatever it is

[12] To apply the label of materialism to the fact (for it *is* a fact) that sense experiences of colors, sounds, tastes have neural bases seems odd. It is not clear just what "dealing with" those qualitative experiences involves. Materialism, I would think, more properly characterizes the program of *identifying* experiences with neural bases.

[13] Nor does the property of thought in Spinoza's substance cease to be thought because it shares the same substance as the property of extension. A monistic doctrine of substance with two (in fact, infinite) attributes does not become a substance of only one property or attribute.

[14] David Chalmers discusses property dualism in his *The Conscious Mind. In Search of a Fundamental Theory* (Oxford: Oxford University Press, 1996). See especially pp. 125, 136, 166, 370n2.

that an understanding of the complex neural networks and neural coding explains about sensory and conscious phenomena, I do not think it *explains away* those phenomena.

The temptation to move from explanatory-reduction to status-reduction arises, I suspect, from several sources. One source for Churchland is his dislike of (and perhaps disdain for) the older metaphysics of two substances, especially talk of nonphysical, immaterial entities. For example, in writing about Nagel's essay on bat experiences, Churchland says that nothing in Nagel's account "entails, indeed it no longer even suggests, that something about the bat's sensory states transcends understanding by the physical sciences" (p. 199). He then addresses the question of whether Nagel's account supports the view that mental states are nonphysical.

If one hopes to argue, then, that mental states have nonphysical features, one needs a better argument than Nagel's. It is of course possible that mental states do have phenomenological features. And it remains possible that one's autoconnected epistemic pathways are precisely what detect them, which is essentially what Nagel is insisting. These ideas are certainly not impossible. Quite the contrary. But their credentials as default assumptions have now evaporated. The mere existence of autoconnected epistemic pathways, which almost every creature possesses. should no longer even suggest the existence of nonphysical features. If they do exist, it is the burden of some other argument to spotlight them. (p. 200)

The existence of nonphysical states can only be established by argument. Why would anyone think that the existence of autoconnected epistemic pathways in the brain would suggest the existence of nonphysical features? Apparently, Churchland thinks there are only two ways to establish the existence of nonphysical features: by pathways in the brain suggesting their existence or by use of some argument. Another source leading some writers to identify conscious phenomena with neural structures is their interest in and knowledge of neuroscientific research. Great progress has been made in neural mapping, in locating and understanding the intricate nature of the brain. The potential for dealing with mental defects through these latest developments in neuroscience (especially when linked with DNA research) is exciting and very promising. Both writers I have discussed have made important contributions, in Hardin's case, to our knowledge and understanding of color perception and the status of colors; in Churchland's case, by many fascinating suggestions about the neural underlay of consciousness.

There is a third possible source for the tendency to blur the distinction between conscious phenomena and neural structure: the language employed to describe the workings of the brain. While seventeenth- and eighteenth-century writers often used physical metaphors and analogies when describing mental phenomena, our contemporary writers apply mental or cognitive terms when referring to brain activity. We have become accustomed to the use of the concept of information applied to computers and other electronic machines. To speak of the brain as processing information need not imply any conscious or epistemic activity.[15] The way a computer or our brain processes input information is not the same as my processing the information about neural networks in Churchland's book. My brain can be said to analyze incoming information from my eyes and my thought processes as I struggle to understand what Churchland describes. Without the neural analysis, my understanding would not occur. It is the explicit application of cognitive language to the neural processing that I find curious, perhaps even misleading. Churchland occasionally speaks cautiously of "cognitive-like processes" in recurrent networks (p. 171), or of the brain's intended bodily behavior (placing the word "intended" in quotation marks, p. 93). Often, he is more explicit. His description of what he identifies as "the general model of cognition being explored in this book" is given in terms of brain functions only:

The brain's global trajectory, through its own neuronal-activation space, follows the well-oiled prototypical pathways that prior learning has carved out in that space; and the brain's global trajectory shifts from one prototype to another as an appropriate function of the brain's changing perceptual inputs. (pp. 171–2)

Elsewhere he speaks of "autoconnected epistemic pathways" in the brain (p. 200), the system of such pathways has a "cognitive grasp of the past" (p. 216), the networks are said to attend to events in the brain, that attention "is steerable by the networks' own cognitive activity" (p. 218). Later, the neural networks are said to "have automatic and certain

---

[15] For a recent example (by a practicing neuroscientist) of the use of the concept of information applied to the brain, see Gillet, *Representation*. He speaks of "the information-processing capacity of the brain" (p. 49). Gillet does go a bit further later in his book, referring to the brain's "cognitive processes" (p. 68). This way of speaking about brain activity has even invaded science reporting. In an article in *The New York Times* for October 13, 1998, "Placebos Prove So Powerful Even Experts Are Surprised," the reporter, Sandra Blakselee, refers to a new field of neuropsychology and its "expectancy theory." That theory, she explains, deals with "what the brain believes about the immediate future" (p. F4). The "brain's expectation" is also mentioned.

knowledge of their own cognitive activities" (p. 319). The brain is even said to be conscious (p. 252).[16]

So with this last remark, is Churchland after all agreeing with Locke's suggestion about thought as a property of the brain? It may be so, but I am not sure that the various terms he ascribes to the brain – conscious, cognitive, epistemic, knowing, attending – carry the same meaning that we (and Locke) ordinarily accept for such terms. The statement of his model of cognition cited above for such terms does not express what I understand when I say "I believe the fire is out," "I know that rose is a Queen Elizabeth," or even "I see the red car in the driveway." I am willing to take Churchland's assurance that when I believe, know or see, my "brain's global trajectory shifts from one prototype to another," but those global trajectories do not describe my *experience* of believing, knowing, or seeing. So when he says the brain is conscious, I think he means something quite different from when I am conscious or aware of what he says. "Know," "believe," "see" and other such words designate actions which are to be described in phenomenological (with trepidation, I say introspective) terms, not global trajectories in the brain.

III

Transferring these psychological terms to brain activity makes it easy for Churchland to slip from explanatory reduction to full-status reduction. That transference of cognitive terms also enables him to avoid a question that troubled the seventeenth- and eighteenth-century philosophers: "how can physicality cause mental events?" Churchland raises this very question while criticizing Nagel's talk of mental states as nonphysical.[17] How could the neural pathways, he asks, "interact with any nonphysical goings-on" (p. 200). The implied answer is, they could not.

---

[16] Jeff Coulter finds this use of terms such as "understand," "recognize," etc., applied to the brain a pervasive practise among present-day cognitivists: they "routinely reify and homogenize the properties of mental and experiential predicates" ("Neural Cartesianism: Comments on the Epistemology of the Cognitive Sciences", in *The Future of the Cognitive Revolution*, ed. David Martel Johnson and Christina E. Erneling, New York: Oxford University Press, 1997, p. 294). Coulter characterizes this merger as a fallacy, "the fallacy of treating 'recognizing' and 'understanding' as predicable of someone's brain, when they are person-level predicates" (p. 293). More generally, cognitivists "conceive of 'perceptions' as 'neural representations' arrived at via 'computations on sensory inputs' (Gregory, Marr), 'memories' as neurally encoded traces, 'engrams' 'representations' of experiences (Booth, Deutsch), 'understanding' as a neural-computational 'process' (Fodor, Chomsky), 'imagining (something rotating)' as 'mentally rotating a neurally-realized image' (Shepard), and so on" (p. 297).

[17] The reference is to Thomas Nagel's famous essay, "What Is It Like to Be a Bat?", *Philosophical Review*, 8, no.4 (1974).

Malebranche and Leibniz of course agreed and accordingly advanced occasionalism and pre-established harmony respectively as solutions. Locke and others freely admitted they did not know how physical processes caused ideas (mental contents). If Churchland were to accept a distinction, as he seems to in some of his remarks, between mental phenomena and their neural analogs, then he could recognize, as Hardin does, the need for two different languages or vocabularies: a language applicable to the phenomena (with the usual epistemic and psychological terms such as "see," "hear," "feel," "believe," "know," "aware," "attend") and another language appropriate for characterizing neural action, structures and pathways. He could still use the first language, or some of it, in the account of neural activity, but he would then have to be explicit about that use being metaphorical when so applied. I am unable to determine, on the basis of his 1995 book, whether he would accept these two languages or two sets of vocabularies.

There is, however, one very curious example he uses that strongly suggests that he ignores the first language (the phenomenal language) while appropriating its epistemic vocabulary. The example, a thought experiment actually, is taken from Frank Jackson.[18] It is another way of posing Nagel's question about "what's it like to be a bat?" Jackson presents a neuroscientist named Mary who has had no color experience, no sensations of color, her world is strictly black and white.[19] Mary has never seen the color red, or had a sensation of that color. The question for Churchland is: "would she know what it is like to see red?" (p. 201). There may be some ambiguity about Churchland's use of this hypothetical example. He phrases Jackson's question both as "what is it like to see red?" and "what is it like actually to have a normal visual sensation of red?" It is not clear from his account whether he takes these two expressions to be the same. Is "seeing red" the same as "having the sensation of red"? I think he wants to draw a distinction between these expressions, a distinction which he believes enables him to use the second phrase to his advantage. Notice how he continues in this passage. Being a neuroscientist, Mary "has learned everything there is to know about the nature of the human visual system and about the way in which the brain discriminates and represents colors" (p. 201). Jackson concludes

[18] "Epiphenomenal Qualia," *Philosophical Quarterly*, 32 (1982).
[19] Churchland suggests that we could think of Mary having her eyes tampered with in order to achieve the same black-and-white result: "I prefer the version where Mary's eyes have high-tech chronic implants that flatten any spectral diversity in the incoming light. The only energy variations that get through to her retina are uniform across the entire spectrum" (p. 200).

that such a person would not know what it is like to see red, and thus there are limits to what physical science can tell us about conscious experience. Churchland challenges that conclusion. Mary, as a trained neuroscientist, Churchland says, is familiar with the sensation of red in other people (in their brains): "she's seen it a thousand times before in the autoconnected pathways of others" (p. 202). What Mary is familiar with on Churchland's account is the sensation of red, not the experience of seeing red. The sensation of red, the sensory state of red is identified by Churchland as a "70–20–30–Hertz coding triplet across the neurons of area V4"! The sensation of red turns out to be a state of the brain. A very strange notion of red and of seeing red. The ambiguity between "seeing red" and "having a sensation of red" thus leaves us with two interpretations. The implied answer to the question Churchland puts, "does Mary know what it is like to see red?," would seem to be, in seeing the autoconnected pathways, Mary sees red! Is the other alternative any better, that Mary knows what it is like to have the sensation of red just by seeing the "70–20–30–Hertz coding triplet across the neurons of area V4"? This alternative strikes me as equally strange. When I have the sensation of red, I am not aware of neural events. To have the sensation of red is, I would think, to see red. So the conclusion should be that Mary definitely does not know what it is like to see red, nor does she know what it is like to have a sensation of red. What she knows is, at best, what is going on in a specific area of the brain when someone sees red or has the visual sensation of red. What Churchland opposes is a claim that what we see when we see red is a nonphysical quality. Hence his translation of seeing the red of a tomato into seeing the behavior of neural pathways.[20]

There is a distinction used by Churchland that he may think preserves the difference between phenomenal experience and brain processes, while avoiding the acceptance of any nonphysical ascription to sense qualia. He gives a number of examples of first-person *ways of knowing* about features of our own body, e.g., knowing the position of our limbs, the congestion in our lungs, the tension of certain muscles. The *object* of

---

[20] He does something similar with examples of light and heat, ignoring seen light and felt heat. "From the standpoint of uninformed common sense, light and its manifold sensory properties certainly seemed to be utterly different from anything so esoteric and alien as coupled electric and magnetic fields oscillating at a million billion cycles per second. And yet, the intuitive impression of vast differences notwithstanding, that is exactly what light turns out to be" (p. 206). It would be instructive to learn what he thinks the status of "seemings" is. They do not exist? For a similar treatment of heat, of the heat we feel when we open an oven door, see p. 207.

such first-person knowledge is something physical: limbs, lungs or muscles. From this, Churchland concludes: "The existence of a proprietary, first-person epistemological access to some phenomenon does not mean that the accessed phenomenon is nonphysical in nature" (p. 198). How does that conclusion apply to my knowledge or awareness of the sensation of red when I look at a rose or a tomato? The mode of awareness of the sensation or even of the sense qualia is first-personal, so Churchland wants to say that that knowledge or awareness also does not give us a nonphysical object, the sense qualia. He wants to say the object of this *way of knowing* is also physical, at least that its first-person status need not mean I am aware of something nonphysical. I am not concerned to defend saying that sense qualia are nonphysical. I do not think that is the important issue. The issue is, is what I know or am aware of when I have a sensation of red or the sensation of heat a specific state of my physical brain? Since Churchland has decided (in his status-reduction mood) that all that there is are physical states and events,[21] he is able to say that while the first-person way of knowing does differ (in kind?) from the scientific way of knowing, the objects are the same for both, i.e., states of autoconnected neural pathways.

Of course, even Mary's "seeing" the sensation of red in the brains of other people (that is, her "seeing" brain events) involves sense qualia, the images on an MRI scanner or on the screen of some more advanced machine, or I suppose, on some other kind of machine that records the electrical–chemical processes of that area of the brain. Those sense qualia indicate (Churchland writes "show") activity in specific areas of the brain. If Churchland wants to say that in seeing such images, in being aware of such sense qualia on the screen of some scanning machine, I am in effect really seeing a "70–20–30–Hertz coding triplet across the neurons of area V4," I guess he is free to do so. But we should be quite clear: what Mary sees visually is a visual shape. Similarly, when I have the sensation of red while looking at a red tomato, I am in fact seeing a tomato. I see the tomato by having visual experiences of shape and color (along with tactile, olfactory, gustatory) qualia. It is the status of these sense qualities that Churchland ignores. Such qualia are present in my experiences as well as in Mary's, in mine when I look at a tomato, in hers when she examines the pictures on an MRI scan of the activity

---

[21] I do not know how Churchland decides what there is. When he writes against Nagel, he says, as we saw, that, at least for the claim that there are nonphysical (immaterial, in an older language) items (e.g., mental states), an *argument* would be needed (p. 200).

in my brain. In being aware of colors, shapes, textures, etc., I am aware of certain objects that possess those qualities.[22] When Mary is aware of whatever is on the screen or dial of some machine, because of her neuroscientific training, she is aware of the electrical–chemical activity in that area of the brain. What she sees on the screen are not qualities or properties of the brain. But Churchland seems to suggest that in ordinary cases of seeing *and* in Mary's seeing, the object of the seeing is not the visual features, the visual shapes and motions. To say that the object of my seeing (in having the sensation of a red, round shape) is not a tomato or the sense qualia I ascribe to a tomato, but some action in the brain, strikes me as a most strange way of speaking. Forget about the issue that seems to worry Churchland – are those sense qualia nonphysical? – and turn to what Hardin calls for, to some phenomenological description. Even more to the point, just recognize that the seemings and appearances, the visual images and tactual feelings, are parts or features of the world we experience.

IV

The eighteenth-century concept of matter as force and power, an active as opposed to the older passive corpuscular concept, made it easier for philosophers to merge thought with brain action. That merging did not turn thought (mentality) into neural action. It may not be very clear what it means to say thought is a property of the brain, the concept of "property of" may need analysis. Spinoza, who was attacked for being a materialist, is the prime example of one who presented an ontology of multiple properties belonging to one subject (substance). The other route taken by eighteenth-century writers making matter itself dynamic and active also makes room for different kinds of properties belonging to one subject. Spinoza's multiple properties, each reflecting the nature of the substance to which they belong, express the nature of the substance from the point of view and in terms of the kind of property each is. There is a parallelism between the properties in much the way that mental action and physical action on Leibniz's account reflect each other and work in tandem.

Churchland speaks of neural analogs to the intrinsic and causal prop-

---

[22] I am trying to avoid the question of whether the sense qualia are qualities of objects. I am also trying to avoid the more difficult question of whether the object is something over and above the qualities I perceive. These are important questions but they are not, I think, germane to the issue raised by Churchland's discussion.

erties of mental states. If such analogs can be found, he thinks that settles the question: mental states will then be physical states.[23] Since thought for Spinoza reflects everything that extension does, it is as if thought could be disposed of and done without. Even more striking, thought would turn out to *be* extension. If property X is the analog of property Y, property Y is really property X! You start with what you take to be two different states, one mental with intrinsic and causal features, the other neural, presumably with its own intrinsic and causal properties. Suddenly, when it is discovered that the neural states are the analogs in all respects of the mental states, it turns out that we did not after all have two different states. A conjuror's trick?

Churchland may not have intended to say that under those conditions mental states disappear, only that we can learn all we need to know about mentality from the neural mechanisms: everything (under the best of conditions) except the experiences of seeing, hearing, feeling, thinking, reasoning. Churchland has the neuroscientist, Mary, seeing, but he offers no account of her visual experiences. He allows her to acquire information from her visual experiences, information about the subject's experience, an experience that also is not analyzed.

I do not want to belabor the obvious, that visual experiences of seeing red roses are not the same as, though tightly correlated with and dependent on, neural processes. What I want to do now is to examine in a brief way the important question raised by Churchland and that worried many seventeenth- and eighteenth-century writers: how can physicality affect mental processes and conscious experiences?

---

[23] The *New York Times* article referred to in note 15 above identifies a thought as "a set of neurons firing," confusing the neural analog with the actual thought processes. In that article, Dr. Howard Fields, a neuroscientist at the University of California at San Francisco, says "We are misled by dualism or the idea that mind and body are separate." The suggestion seems to be that "separate" means "distinct and unrelated." Mind and body can be separate, even distinct, but closely related, as Descartes insisted. The *New York Times* science section for January 5, 1999, carries a heading for an article: "Using Magnets on Corners of the Mind," but the first sentence of the article speaks of "surgical instruments inserted in the brain." No mention of mind in the article.

2

Causing and signifying

> . . . why could nature not . . . have established some sign which
> would make us have the sensation of light . . . it is our mind which
> represents to us the idea of light each time our eye is affected by the
> action which signifies it.
>
> Descartes, Le monde, ch. 1

I want to explore the question of the relation between perceiving objects
and the role objects play in perception. I shall examine several recent
articles and books which deal with this relation. I do so against the background of seventeenth- and eighteenth-century discussions of that relation and of the nature of perception. The causal theory of perception
is often associated with some of the writers in those centuries.[1] The
causal theory of perception says that objects (and their actions) cause us
to perceive them. Presumably the claim is more than merely that I perceive the desk when certain physical events (light rays, electrical and
chemical events) occur; there is more than concomitance and correlation. The theory says that the physical processes (events) from object to
nerves and brain are necessary and are *parts of* the cause of conscious
perception. The nature of the causal process is usually explicated by the
physical sciences: physics, chemistry and optics. But my *experience* of perceiving the desk is not itself one of the physical events in this process. So
we need to ask "what is the total set of necessary and sufficient conditions for perception?"

There does not seem to be an account of the causation of sense *experience*, other than the account of what happens in nerves and brain, but
events in nerves and brain are not the experience of seeing a desk, or
even of being aware of sense qualities. Physical causation seems to some
philosophers incapable of "causing" my seeing, no matter how impor-

---

[1] For a discussion of these earlier writers, see my *Perceptual Acquaintance* (1984) and *Perception and
Reality* (1996).

tant and necessary that causation is for my seeing or feeling. Recognition of this feature of perception, of the difference between seeing, feeling, hearing and the neurophysiological correlates, a feature that many of our contemporaries want to deny, led some seventeenth- and eighteenth-century philosophers to deny any causal relation between the physical world of desks, trees, stones and our being aware of or perceiving those objects.[2] Some settled for correlation (occasionalism or pre-established harmony) and let it go at that. Often, these writers had metaphysical and theological reasons which reinforced (or forced) their denial of a causal relation. Some medical men in eighteenth-century France, operating on brain-damaged soldiers, discovered some specific correlations between damaged areas in the brain and sensory impairment.[3] Even more specific correlations were suggested for thinking and perceiving. Other writers, philosophers, in those centuries accepted the difference between brain events and experiences of seeing and touching; they seemed to accept the notion of a causal relation for those experiences, but they admitted that they had no idea how that causation worked. A few writers suggested (as Descartes does in the quotation at the head of this chapter) that the physical causal relation between objects in the physical world was supplemented by a different kind of relation, a *sign relation*, where the same physical events that bring about physical events in nerves and brain also (with the help of brain motion as signs to the mind) bring about experiences of seeing tables, hearing church bells, smelling the scent of roses. This second "bring about" relation was modeled on the way written marks on paper or spoken words result in our understanding what is written or what is said. The ink marks on paper or the sounds in the air cause physical events in a reader's or listener's nerves and brain, but they also "cause" us to take those marks or sounds as words in a language: we both hear the sounds and understand what is said.

Is there a parallel between language acquisition and the acquisition of ideas (the seventeenth-century term), or sensory mental contents? The child seems to see colors and shapes, to hear sounds; conscious awareness, as different from bodily reaction and neural activity, occurs early,

---

[2] In the passage I cited in the previous chapter, where Churchland criticized Nagel's argument for nonphysical features in experience, Churchland adds: "even if such nonphysical features were to exist, why should one's autoconnected pathways pay any attention to them?" As I noted in the previous chapter, he follows this up with another question: "How could they interact with any nonphysical goings-on?" This is a rather typical reaction.

[3] For a brief discussion, see *Locke and French Materialism* (1991), pp. 101–9.

even pre-natally, and without any obvious learning process. When the infant begins to discriminate specific colors, shapes, sounds and later acquires the idea of objects (even absent objects), that perceptual success is closely accompanied by language learning. Both the acquisition of language and the awareness of sensory qualities and objects take place in a context of language users and perceivers. How an understanding of words is achieved, how the child acquires a language, is itself not fully understood. Various theories have been advanced involving innate or built-in mechanisms. Presumably these mechanisms, even if they take the form of innate language abilities (a language of thought), must work with the sounds and neural apparatus to "produce" a non-neural response. A translation of neural events into linguistic events takes place, whether the translation is a function of the postulated innate language skills or is traced to the brain.

The sign-relation in sense perception mentioned by Descartes seems to follow the language model fairly closely. Language acquisition cannot be divorced from the neural mechanism. Neural activity is even more central to the perception of objects and qualities. Some recent writers, addressing questions of perception, speak of the brain as both a physical mechanism and a semantic or syntactic machine (engine). Earlier versions of this notion of translation from physical to nonphysical events can be found in those scholastic theories that talked of an agent intellect as the source of the translation from sensible (physical) species entering the body of the perceiver into intelligible (nonphysical, immaterial, cognitive) species. Later philosophers distinguished the mind from the body, making the mind, not the brain, the interpreter of incoming signals to the body. Descartes may have been the first to identify neural action (motions in nerves and brain caused by physical objects external to the body) as signs to the mind of those external objects. Glanvill, Cudworth and Bonnet employed the same suggestion, with a few additions.[4] The claim was that the mind was of such a nature that it interpreted (transformed) the neural action as meaningful signs. The neural action was both physical and the bearer of meaning; motion in the brain carries information about the external world. Neither the scholastic agent intellect nor the interpreter mind for Descartes was anything like the "little

[4] For a discussion of the sign theory, see *Perceptual Acquaintance*, chs. 1 and 11, and *Perception and Reality*, ch. 8. Species and ideas as signs were prominent in late scholasticism, but I do not know if anyone ever talked of brain states or motions as signs. See John Deely, *New Beginnings: Early Modern Philosophy and Postmodern Thought* (Toronto: University of Toronto Press, 1994), and Robert Pasnau, *Theories of Cognition in the Later Middle Ages* (Cambridge: Cambridge University Press, 1997). I am indebted to David Behan for calling these two important studies to my attention.

man in the brain" that our contemporaries like to charge against such theories. The agent intellect and the Cartesian mind are just features of the person which function in the way described.

Nevertheless, those functions are not disconnected from the neurophysiological mechanisms of the body. That mechanism in sensory awareness is put into action by physical events coming from the object and the environment. The perceiver as a physical organism clearly stands in a causal relation with the environment, with the objects that impinge on bodily organs. The question is: "is the perceiver as conscious person also in a causal relation with external objects?" Of even more pressing concern, "what precisely is the role of the internal neural mechanism in conscious perception?" These two questions in various forms have a long tradition among philosophers. They have been intertwined with issues of realism (direct or indirect), knowledge and skepticism, the very nature and status of consciousness, experience and awareness, and the more recent discussions of mental causation.

I

Frank Jackson finds it incredible that there could be two different kinds of causation between the physical world and our awareness of that world.[5] More precisely, for in that article he was not addressing the topic of perception, what he finds incredible is "that mental to physical causation is different in kind from physical to physical causation."[6] Part of the reason Jackson finds this suggestion incredible is that it requires "an interactionist dual attribute metaphysics." The fact that he speaks of dual *attributes*, not two *substances*, is significant, but neither sort of dualism is acceptable to him (or to many other of our contemporaries). Jackson wants to retain the notion of mental causation, but he does so by identifying mental states with physical (brain) states.[7] Once that merger is accomplished, it becomes incredibly easy to say mental to physical causation is the same as physical to physical causation. On those terms, mental causation *is* physical causation. He wants to know "where in the physical story the mental states are," that is, where mental states are

---

[5] "Mental Causation," *Mind*, 105, no. 419 (July 1996), p. 387.

[6] For perception, the two causal relations are physical to physical and physical to mental, but I assume Jackson would find it equally incredible to say these differ in kind.

[7] His account is given under the "transparency assumption": "whatever we say about mental causation must make perfect sense when viewed in terms of what the physical sciences say about the causation of behavior" (p. 379). It is *behavior*, changes of body position and location, that Jackson wants to explain.

located, located not just in a story, but their physical location (p. 387). His explication of "why the brain is the plausible place to locate mental states" is, I think, rather curious but probably typical of many other writers today.

> Consider what happens when I enter a room and acquire the belief that there is a pot of coffee on the table, which then leads me to move towards the table. My belief is something that happens to me as a result of my body's change of situation in the world, which [belief?] then affects the movements of my body in certain distinctive ways. So, in order to locate the belief, we need to ask for the location of the crucial changes consequent on my change of situation that affect how my body moves. (p. 387)

Those crucial changes "are somewhere in the brain" (p. 388).

   Notice the progression in this passage:
(a) I enter the room.
(b) I acquire the belief.
(c) The belief leads me to move.
The passage then offers an account of belief acquisition:
(d) The belief happens to me.
(e) The belief is a result of my body's change of place.
(f) The belief affects the movement of my body towards the table.
(g) Certain changes in the brain are consequent on the body's change of
     place.
Since "it is a discovery of science that unless the brain changes in certain ways, subjects do not acquire beliefs, and their behavior is not affected in the ways distinctive of beliefs," he concludes that the belief is (also?) located in the brain (p. 388).

   A number of remarks need to be made on this passage. Are we to read the phrase "consequent on" in step (g), and the term "affects" in step (f) as causal terms? Does the body's change of place, a change of location in the world (from outside the room to inside) cause certain brain events, and do these new brain events cause the body to move towards the table? Does the phrase in (d), "happens to me," combined with "result of" in (e), indicate another causal relation? I am passive in acquiring a belief, the action of my body in changing places causes the belief. Once I enter the room, the causal sequences unfold, *my entering* the room seems only incidental to what happens. It is *my body*, its change of place and its motion that initiate the changes in the brain. Since those changes in the brain affect how my body moves towards the coffee table, the belief is also located in the brain. In fact, Jackson wants to say that those changes in the brain *are* the belief that there is coffee in the room. There are not two brain states. Ordinarily, we do not think of belief as a brain state, so on Jackson's account, the ordinary belief that there is coffee in the room (and my desire to have some) is out of the causal loop, it plays no (causal) role in my heading for the coffee on the table. It is all accomplished through body location, body movement and brain changes. Is this what it means to identify belief with brain states?

Not only does the ordinary belief that there is coffee in the room seem to disappear, the person designated by "I," "me" and "my" drops out of the account, to be replaced by the body and the brain.[8] Despite the fact that the passage starts with a reference to "when I enter the room," not "when my body enters the room," and despite the apparent distinction between what happens to me and what happens to my body, the "me" seems to be replaced by "my body," and any reference to "I change or move" becomes "the body changes or moves." It is, I would think, Jackson (the "I," the "me") that acquires the belief, not his brain. What is left out of this account is the fact that the person has to see the objects in the room, has to smell the coffee, has to know and understand what coffee is – just to mention a few of the items involved. If the "subject" has not grown up in a society, has not acquired a language, has not become aware of objects via his senses, does not find the smell of coffee attractive, no brain states will be able to cause him to move towards the coffee. These various cognitive skills are also crucial for the acquisition or formation of the belief that there is coffee in the room. When I form that belief and my body moves towards the table, it does so because *I* move it. The events in the brain are necessary for the action of moving towards the table, but so are the cognitive events, the events of seeing, hearing, smelling, desiring, understanding. These latter events may be consequent to the neural events, but that hardly makes them the same as the neural events. The interesting question is: "what is the nature of the relation between the antecedent and the consequent, between the brain state and the states or processes of seeing, hearing, smelling, etc.?"

II

In some of the most recent writings on perception, this question has been addressed. E. J. Lowe thinks that "any remotely plausible theory of

---

[8] I called attention in the previous chapter to Churchland's use of cognitive terms to characterize brain processes. The result was the illusion that consciousness, knowing, perceiving and the person are not needed. The disappearance of the person, the perceiver, is, I think, rather typical of much contemporary discussion. See my *Perception and Reality*, pp. 37–40, and chapter 3 below.

perception must be a 'causal' theory," in the sense that there must be an "appropriate" causal relation between perceptual experience and the object perceived.[9] The causal relation is between the experience and some of the properties of the object. It is the sensuous features of experience that stand in a causal relation to the object. Lowe raises the question of what is the precise nature of that causal relation (causal dependency, he says). His answer is that it is a systematic, functional relation.[10] In a more recent article, Lowe speaks of perceptual experience being caused "in an appropriate sort of way by a process originating in the object perceived."[11] The appropriate way is a systematic co-variance between properties of the object and qualitative features of our experience. He reaffirms there that what is caused are the sensuous features, the qualia, of our perceptual experience.[12] In another essay, Lowe describes vision as involving "a certain kind of *responsiveness*" to the objects, or as "a special kind of causal dependency."[13] In that same place, he goes on to use the notion of "being affected" by objects.

What I say is that visual experiences have to be affected by certain properties of the seen object *in such a fashion* that the observer is thereby enabled to form a fairly reliable judgment as to what those properties are. Even so, I can and should try to say what would qualify an effect upon visual experience as apt for the role it is here called upon to play. Two questions in particular arise: first, *what* features of visual experience need to be affected by an object if one is to see it, and second, how do these features need to be affected.[14]

Again, it is the phenomenal qualities that are the result of being affected; the relation between those phenomenal qualities and properties of the object may be causal, but Lowe selects the word "affected" instead of "caused." Is this because he wants to distinguish that relation

---

[9] "Perception: A Causal Representative Theory," in *New Representationalisms: Essays in the Philosophy of Perception*, ed. Edmond Wright, p. 142. This article has been incorporated into Lowe's *Subjects of Experience* (Cambridge: Cambridge University Press, 1996).   [10] *Ibid.*, pp. 143–45.

[11] In his *Locke on Human Understanding* (London: Routledge, 1995), p. 59.

[12] *Ibid.*, pp. 60–1. In his essay in *New Representationalisms*, Lowe is careful to deny any causal relation between objects and our beliefs or judgments: "we are not directly caused by the objects we perceive, to have perceptual experiences *with such-and-such intentional* objects, only to have perceptual experiences *with such-and-such sensuous features*." (p. 145)

[13] "Experience and its Objects," in *The Contents of Experience: Essays on Perception*, ed. Tim Crane (Cambridge: Cambridge University Press, 1992), pp. 82–3. This article has also been incorporated into Lowe's *Subjects of Experience*.

[14] *Ibid.*, p. 83. Lowe may not have Kant in mind with this talk of being affected by the object, but there are some tantalizing uses of what Kant calls the affection relation in his *Critique of Pure Reason*. For Kant, that relation seems to be a noncausal relation. For a discussion of the affection relation in Kant, and how it relates to perception and questions about realism, see Moltke S. Gram's *The Transcendental Turn: The Foundation of Kant's Idealism* (Gainsville: University of Florida Press, 1984) and my *Perception and Reality*, ch. 7.

from the physical causal relation between objects and nerves and brain?

I cannot determine whether Lowe's use of the terms "affected," "responsiveness" and "appropriate" reflect any uncertainty on his part about ascribing a causal relation between objects and perceptual experience. Perhaps not, since in his book on Locke he characterizes the systematic co-variance of the relation as causal power.[15] Does he mean that co-variance indicates causal power? Or is the causal power in addition to the co-variance? If the former, if co-variance is what he means by causal power, the notion of power seems to disappear, to sink into co-variance. If the latter, if there is co-variance as well as causal power, then we need some analysis of the power. He does not offer any analysis of how that causal power works, how it might differ from the power of objects to bring about changes in sense organs, nerves and brain.

A difference is suggested by another writer, Howard Robinson, who explores various answers to the question of "how a distal stimulus could be experienced as subjective content," or "how the existence of an external causal connection can be experienced as an internal content."[16] In a brief discussion of David Armstrong, Robinson draws an important distinction "between the immediate causal output of a brain process – which will be a small electric charge – and its causal significance for the behavior of the organism as a whole."[17] Robinson does not explain the difference but the suggestion is, I think, that it is relevant to understanding the sequence of events from the object to sense organs, to nerves and brain, and to conscious awareness. The causal output applies to nerves and brain, the causal significance applies to awareness.

III

Robinson does not say enough about that distinction to enable me to know how he would analyze the *significance* of the causal process. Grant Gillett is more explicit in his *Representation, Meaning and Thought*. To understand and explain human behavior, we need more than just a causal history, we need "mental or meaningful explanations."[18] He was writing about a schizophrenic patient, but he points out that we often use such explanations in our normal, everyday life as well. Such explanations "illuminate the relation between the agent concerned and his world in such a way as to make sense of his actions. And it is not at all clear that

---

[15] *Locke on Human Understanding*, pp. 191–2.
[16] Howard Robinson, "Physicalism, Externalism and Perceptual Representation," in *New Representationalisms*, pp. 109, 108. [17] *Ibid.*, p. 110. [18] *Representation, Meaning and Thought*, p. 72.

such explanations can be depersonalized in the way that natural causal explanations must be."[19] Meaningful explanations "are not causal or mechanical as are the causal relations in physical sciences." When "the thoughts of a disturbed person become more ordered as he begins to return to normal," it is naïve to explain that change "in terms of the relations between causal sequences in his brain." What has happened, the "essential change is that at a certain time his behavior is not merely caused to occur by states in his brain but begins to make sense, and that reflects a change in his interactions with others and the world." There are two kinds of interactions: a physical, causal interaction and a meaningful or significatory one. Interaction is the basic relation, but some interactions between perceivers and agents and the environment are not physical.

Gillett's general claim is that interaction with other people enables us to acquire and "internalize an essentially public and social set of techniques which organize and make tractable the features of the environment that have been found relevant by their social group."[20] Even the brain is shaped by these interpersonal factors.[21] He insists that "attempts to reduce cognition and mental content to causal transactions are misinformed and misdirected." He makes this claim from his knowledge of work in the cognitive neurosciences. Accounts of sense, meaning and cognitive significance can be given "without invoking causal connections between the subject and his environment."[22] His view stands in rather sharp contrast with a view such as Jackson's, insisting as he does that "the explanation of human behavior goes beyond the antecedent states causing bodily movements."[23]

Gillett does not write about perception directly, but much of his discussion has relevance to perception. He does raise the question which has kept philosophers busy from the seventeenth century to today of "how the contents of our thoughts can rest on properties of the thinker and yet be about things in the world."[24] His answer lies in his notion that the concepts we use help shape the world we know; those concepts are

---

[19] *Ibid.*, p. 73.   [20] *Ibid.*, p. 77.

[21] "Thus exact effects of incoming patterns on brain function are constrained in part by genetically determined structure but critically shaped in the course of experience"(*ibid.*, p. 71). Not just shaped, but structured: "Interactions and experiences have structured those brain processes in such a way as they fulfill a particular informational or causal function" (p. 70).

[22] *Ibid.*, p. 122. Cf. p. 129.

[23] *Ibid.*, p. 99. Even more emphatically: "Given the nature of human beings, the brain and its capacity for information-processing is essential to mental life, but what the brain actually does is dependent on the conceptual structure of the person whose brain it is. There is, therefore, an undischarged explanatory debt in resting mental explanation on brain function" (p. 75).

[24] *Ibid.*, p. 101.

acquired from our relations with other language users and concept users. He offers Kant as an example of this general notion (pp. 7, 56). Of even greater importance is his reference to Kant's account of human action as the result of a different kind of causality (Kant calls it "free causality") from the causality between events.[25] On Kant's account we belong to two realms, the physical or phenomenal realm of our body and the intelligible realm of agents of action. However we interpret the two-realms notion, its importance lies in its recognition that human actions are more than behavior, more than body movements (e.g., towards coffee on the table).[26] As conscious beings, as perceivers and actors, we are, as Gillett reads Kant (correctly), "distinct in important ways from the causal order that surrounds us" (p. 3).

IV

Among our contemporaries, there has been a reluctance (distaste might be more accurate) to accept any form of dualism, whether it be a Kantian two-realms dualism or the earlier two-substance dualism of Descartes and other seventeenth-century writers. There are encouraging signs that this rejection of dualism is gradually disappearing. Two examples are Robinson's distinction between causal output and causal significance, and Gillett's science-based insistence on the difference between brain states and concepts, with his recognition of the difference between body movement and action. The reference to Kant's account of agency is especially important since it can lead to a reinstatement of the person in accounts of perception and awareness. David Chalmers's bold book, *The Conscious Mind,* is another example of a firm recognition of dual processes, physical and phenomenal.

It is of historical interest that Chalmers characterizes the dualism he defends as "property dualism," historically interesting because the substance dualism of the seventeenth century developed into property dualism in the hands of philosophers such as Locke, perhaps Hume, certainly Joseph Priestley, La Mettrie, Holbach and Diderot.[27] This change

---

[25] *Ibid.*, pp. 59–60.
[26] See *ibid.*, p. 64: "it is futile to try and elucidate the essence of an action by looking closely at it as a bodily movement."
[27] For the characterization of Locke's and Priestley's account as property dualism, see my *Thinking Matter.* For that term ascribed to the French writers, see my *Locke and French Materialism,* esp. pp. 207–11. For a definition of property dualism, see Lowe, *Subjects of Experience,* p. 53: "Property dualism (attributed to Spinoza by some commentators) is then the view that mental and physical properties are quite distinct, but may none the less be properties of the same substantial particular – which by some accounts might be the brain (a physical substance)."

happened because of skepticism about our knowledge going beyond experience and observation, as well as from the change in the concept of matter from corpuscular to force and power. For Chalmers, consciousness is not presented directly as a property of the brain, as thought was for Locke in his suggestion about thinking matter. Chalmers does speak of physical and phenomenal properties, but he prefers to speak more generally of consciousness as part of the character or feature of the world (p. 123); it is a feature over and above the physical features (p. 125). Occasionally he speaks of two different kinds of facts about the world. It is clear, however, that for him consciousness is related to the brain. He frequently uses the language of "arises from," consciousness arises from the physical (p. 247). Sometimes it is experience that arises from "the fine-grained functional organization" of a physical system (p. 248; cf. p. 206). The phrase "arises from" sounds causal, as if the brain produces consciousness. But the causal language is softened by Chalmers's use of the current popular buzzword, "supervenience."

There is a large and sometimes somewhat technical literature on the notion of supervenience.[28] I do not know whether Chalmers's account of this term is typical. The ordinary meaning is that of something added to something else, some additional feature or property. The ordinary meaning also has the sense of something extraneous being added. As used by philosophers, it seems to indicate a relation weaker than causal but stronger than correlation. Chalmers's brief definition employs the term "determine": "The notion of supervenience formalizes the intuitive idea that one set of facts can fully determine another set of facts" (p. 32). Sometimes he uses the term "fix": one set of facts fixes another set of facts (pp. 32, 35). Distinguishing logical from natural supervenience, he speaks of "necessitation": one set of facts necessitates another set (p. 37). To help us understand the difference between logical and natural supervenience, he offers a conceptual example (borrowed from Kripke):

If B-properties supervene logically on A-properties, then once God (hypothetically) creates a world with certain A-facts, the B-facts come along for free as an automatic consequence. If B-properties merely supervene naturally on A-properties, however, then after making sure of the A-facts, God has to do more work in order to make sure of the B-facts: he has to make sure there is a law relating the A-facts and the B-facts. (p. 38)

---

[28] For a recent collection of essays on the topic, some rather technical, see *Supervenience: New Essays*, ed. Elias S. Savellos and Ümit D. Yalçin (Cambridge: Cambridge University Press, 1995).

As applied to consciousness, "When God created the world, after ensuring that the physical facts held, *he had more work to do*. He had to ensure that the facts about consciousness held" (p. 124).

This explanation is very similar to the scenario Locke used when he explained his suggestion that God could add thought to suitably organized matter (i.e. the brain). Locke pictures God creating an extended, solid substance and then adding motion to that substance. God could have decided to leave off motion. Sense and life are also added. Then, God creates another substance, an unextended substance (in the terms of the ontology then, an immaterial substance). The question was, should he add thought to that substance? When God added motion, life and sense to the extended substance, the nature of the substance was not changed. Similarly, God could have added thought to that first substance, instead of creating a second substance.[29] In both Locke's example and Chalmers's illustration, thought or consciousness is a property added to the physical. The A-facts for Locke would be the properties of extension and solidity, the B-facts would be the property of thought. On Locke's supposition, we would have one substance with two different kinds of properties, thought and extension. In his example, both motion and thought would be supervenient properties; since they were added later by God, neither was part of the essence of the one substance.

Does designating these properties as supervenient properties help us understand the relation between consciousness and the brain? Saying that, when brain states of a certain sort occur (or when there is a specific organization in the brain), conscious experience will occur, does not tell us much about the relation, even if we can discover natural laws that cover those occurrences. We still are left in the dark about how conscious experience arises out of, or in conjunction with, physical events in the brain. Chalmers's answer is closer to "in conjunction with" than it is to "arises from." He uses the concept of information, suggesting that it is "the key to the fundamental connection between physical processes and conscious life." The physical processes he refers to are located in the brain, either in specific areas or more globally. He uses the locution of "information space" and he speaks of information being "realized" in different media (e.g., in the physical world, the brain and the phenomenal world). I think he accepts the notion that information requires processing (p. 282), but I am not sure about his analysis of that notion. I

---

[29] Locke's *Reply to the Bishop of Worcester's Answer to His Second Letter*, in *Works* (1823), vol. 4, pp. 460–2.

would suppose information must be transmitted or translated (perhaps both) from world to brain to conscious experience. When the information is realized in the brain, it takes a form suitable to the structure and operation of neurons and electrical events. When that same information is realized in a perceptual and phenomenal space, how does that realization take place? Presumably the information comes to be located in my conscious experience (my perceptual field) via its location in the brain. The route from object to brain is marked by physical events (photons, light waves), straightforward physical, causal processes. What kind of process is it that activates or relocates (transmits, translates) the information from brain to perceptual awareness?

Chalmers may not have an answer to that question; it may not be important to him or even relevant to his project. His concern is with finding psychophysical laws linking brain and experience. He suggests several such laws (or principles): a coherence principle, a structural principle, and the principle of organizational invariance (p. 276). These principles are not for him *fundamental*; they express regularities only. I cannot determine whether the fundamental principle or law he seeks must go beyond regularity, or whether it just gives us more specific knowledge about experiences. He says experience arises from the physical, but the way in which information is realized phenomenally in experience is important. That "arises from" relation is not analyzed, so far as I can discover, although he does note that information is realized phenomenally when it is realized physically (in the brain). Regularity again. Is there a processing of information in the brain which turns that information into perceptual terms? Or is it just that the one follows upon the other (or occurs with the other)? Is information another form of Descartes's suggestion of a sign relation between brain and conscious perceivers? What makes the concept of information, or Descartes's brain notions as signs, more fundamental or more intelligible than coherence or invariance?

v

What makes the concept of information important in addressing the relation between brain and mind, or the relation between objects in the world and conscious awareness, is the dual realization it can have: it can be realized in the medium of neurons and electrical–chemical processes; and it can also be realized in phenomenal, perceptual, sensory, qualita-

tive experience.[30] In Chalmers's account we find a modern variant of the
Aristotelian and scholastic notion of the form of objects being able to
reside in matter or in mind. In both the scholastic version and in this
updated twentieth-century version, there is a transfer or translation of
features in the physical environment to conscious awareness. The scholastics were not, I think, much concerned with the neurophysiological
processes in these transfers or translations, but Descartes and other sev-
enteenth- and eighteenth-century philosophers recognized the role
played by events in the brain as an intermediary between the world and
experience. Beyond suggesting that the brain's relation to the mind (consciousness or the person) is a semantic, significatory one, Descartes and
a few others do not explain how we pick up the information encoded in
brain motions. Nor, I think, does Chalmers tell us how the information
realized in the brain becomes information *for me*. We have physical events
and information events, physical media and semantic media, but precisely how information moves from the physical to the semantic (or,
Lowe prefers to say, ideational) media is unexplained.

That there are two interactive relations seems clear: physical to physical (events or processes in the environment causing events in nerves and
brain) and physical to mental (events in the brain that cause or result in
perceivers becoming aware of sense qualia, such as colors, sounds,
tastes). Whether we label both of these "causal" may be less important
than recognizing the difference between the physical events of the first
interactive relation and the awareness feature of the second. It has to be
admitted, however, that neither the talk of a significatory or meaningful
interaction nor the notion of two kinds of causal processes has been
given adequate or detailed analysis. What seems to me to be worth some
attention are the various writers from Descartes and late scholastics, to
other seventeenth- and eighteenth-century elaborations of a sign relation, or to the more recent authors cited in this chapter, who have found
a need to search for a relation between physical events and cognition.

---

[30] John Sutton thinks that, when I wrote in *Perceptual Acquaintance* (p. 18) that Descartes rejected "any
relation between the physical activity of objects on our senses and the perceptual ideas in our
minds," I was distinguishing my semantic interpretation of brain-motion signs from "causal or
information-theoretic accounts, by which corporeal motions encode information about the
external objects which caused them" (*Philosophy and Memory Traces: Descartes to Connectionism*,
Cambridge: Cambridge University Press, 1998, p. 295). If I gave that impression, I would want
to correct it here. One way to understand Descartes's suggestion of natural signs in the brain
can be to say that information is encoded there. But information encoded in the brain still has
to be translated into perceived or conscious information. It is that translation that I have suggested cannot be called "causal" in the usual sense, in the physical sense.

The suggestion of two different kinds of causation, or a causal and a significatory interaction, strikes some as objectionable if not just false. If, as I have tried to do in other discussions, I treated the significatory relation as noncausal, I have done so on the assumption that we think of causal relations in physical terms. The process from brain to mind does not seem to me to be a physical process. Nevertheless, there does seem to be a connection, even an interaction. It *is* difficult to talk of that interaction without using causal words or phrases, such as "gives rise to," "triggers," "stimulated by," "affected." What is required is some analysis of the process from brain to conscious perception, which will differentiate that process from those that occur within the brain itself, or elsewhere in our bodies. There have been traditions where the notion of different kinds of causal relations was accepted (e.g., Aristotelian, Thomistic systems). In some late scholastics, we find talk of signs and of a significatory relation. It may have been those writings that led Descartes to describe brain motions as natural signs. A theory of signs may shed light on the second interactive relation, as Deely has suggested.[31] Thus, there is work to be done.

Part of the reluctance by some writers to accept the notion of a noncausal relation, or even of two different kinds of causal relations, may be due to the desire to naturalize epistemology. Attempts to naturalize tend to lead to some version of materialism; to naturalize epistemology is taken to mean cognition is a function of the brain. Causal processes in the brain, as in the physical world at large, involve such events as electrical–chemical processes, energy transfers or, in earlier times, the motion of corpuscles or animal spirits. Hence, it seems to be assumed, if there is a causal relation between brain and mind, it has to be of this kind of event. By assimilating seeing, perceiving, or awareness to brain events or making them properties of the brain, any need for a second kind of causal relation disappears. Perhaps we can naturalize epistemology and avoid these moves into materialism. The distinction I have tried to draw between two different causal relations or processes may wait upon further analysis, further explication. I think some of the writers I have presented in this chapter do go some way towards such analysis.

There is, I would say, another relation which has a somewhat similar unexplained process, the relation between mind (or the person) and the

---

[31] See Deely's *New Beginnings* and his translation of John of Saint Thomas's *Tractatus de Signis*. David Behan is at work on applying semiotic theory to Descartes's ideas. For a brief essay foreshadowing his important work, see his contribution to a symposium discussion of my reading of Descartes, in *Descartes's Natural Philosophy*, ed. John Sutton and Stephen Gaukroger (forthcoming).

brain, Jackson's mental to physical causation. This relation seems to depend upon the brain-to-body relation. I raise my arm or hand. In doing so, I cause a body motion, the motion of my arm or hand. How do I do that? In raising my arm, I also (perhaps indirectly) cause certain brain events to occur. Or is it that I first cause those brain events to occur and then my arm rises? We certainly are not conscious of causing brain events to occur, but I do seem to know that I raised my arm. The nature of the causal process (if it *is* a causal process) is unknown, unidentified and not described. The mind–brain relation is the inverse of the brain–mind relation, but both seem equally unexplained. The mind-to-brain (and hence to the body) relation is in fact the relation of a person as agent to actions performed, actions such as my raising my arm or repaying a debt. To understand how actions are possible, how they are able to enter into or become parts of physical events, may require us to follow Kant into his concept of two realms. For Kant, the causation involved in the mind-to-body and person-to-action relations was an *initiating* cause, the introduction of a new event into the world, both a new bodily event and a new intentional event (such as a moral action). The person is more than the body, so the category difference is captured by Kant's talk of two realms. Perhaps the status and nature of the person, the agent, the perceiver, the subject may point a way towards understanding these unexplained relations.

3

Actions and persons

> . . . a mans holding a gun in his hand & pulling downe the triger
> may be either Rebellion, Parricide, Murther, Homicide, Duty,
> Justice, Valor or recreation & be thus variously diversified when all
> the circumstances put together are compard to a rule, though the
> simple action of holding the gun & pulling the triger may be exactly
> the same.
>
> John Locke, Draft A of the Essay, §23

> Kant says "Thoughts without content are empty, intuitions without
> concepts are blind." Similarly, intentions without overt activity are
> idle, and movements of limbs without concepts are mere happen-
> ings, not expressions of agency.
>
> John McDowell, Mind and World, p. 89.

So far, I have discussed the first two contrasts on my list: appearance and
reality *and* phenomena and causes. The first chapter used Paul
Churchland's preferences for reality (neural networks) over the visible
phenomena which give us access to dials, images and lines which in turn
are taken as evidence of nonvisible neural events. Theory, predictions
and explanations afforded by them, in Churchland's analysis, tend to
divert attention from the relevant phenomena. For the purposes of the
view he defends, phenomena are of lesser value than the neural structures and events. The person, both of the investigator and of the subject
of experiments (as with the example of Mary the neuroscientist), seems
also to be ignored. The person seems to me to be missing from other contemporary writings on cognition and perception.[1] If we are interested in
what Hume characterized as the "science of man," or if we want to
include all of the relevant ingredients in our account of the world we
know and experience, we need to find a way of saving the appearances

---

[1] See my discussion of J. J. Valberg's *The Puzzle of Experience* (1993), in my *Perception and Reality*, pp.
36–41.

along with the person. We need to make room in our ontology for both appearances and reality. At least, we need to do so if we believe ontology has a place in our philosophy, not exactly a priority among philosophers today.

Once we take on this task, a pressing problem for us as well as for those in the eighteenth century is the relation between reality and appearance. More specifically, we need to reach an understanding of how physical events can cause or result in mental events. Chapter 2 discussed some recent writings where the authors recognize that physical causation may be incompatible with cognitive events. Descartes made a passing suggestion about a sign relation between brain motion and ideas. Cognitive events seem clearly to be dependent on neural processes, indirectly on physical events in the environment. But what is the nature of that dependence? The relation between physical processes in the brain and conscious experience is an intimate, dependent relation, but the details of the transformation from neural events to our awareness of colors, sounds, shapes and perhaps physical objects are difficult to discover or even to formulate in theory.

We can perhaps fill in one of the gaps in that transformation if we are able to characterize the status, the ontological status, of appearances. Do they have an existence between physical and mental? Clarifying the status of appearances may also help secure a place for them in accounts of perception and reality. I want to suggest in this chapter a way of considering appearances which gives them a status similar to that of actions and persons. We are now ready for the third and fourth items on my five-fold list.

I

A decade or so ago, philosophers turned their attention to the concept of action. Many books and articles were published on that concept.[2] One of the distinctions drawn is between bodily motion, such as the movement of an arm, and my moving my arm. E. J. Lowe has recently characterized this distinction as between bodily motion and bodily movement, where the latter has an implied relation to a self or person,

---

[2] My entry into those discussions is contained in a series of articles: "Ascriptions, Descriptions, and Action Sentences," *Ethics* 67 (July 1957): 307–10; "Act and Circumstance," *Journal of Philosophy* 59, no. 13 (June 21, 1962): 337–50; "Agent Causality," *American Philosophical Quarterly* 3 (1966): 14–26; "My Hand Goes out to You," *Philosophy* 41, no. 156 (April 1966): 140–52; "Action: Metaphysic and Modality," *American Philosophical Quarterly* 10 (April 1973): 71–85; "Action Theory as the Foundation for the Sciences of Man," *Philosophy of the Social Sciences* 3 (1973): 81–90.

to an actor.[3] There is still another distinction within action, the difference between my moving my arm and my bidding at an auction, my signalling a turn in my car. Once we understand that *an action*, such as repaying a debt or telling the truth, is in some way different from the bodily motion on which it rides, we may find a way to integrate into one ontology perceiving (being aware) and actions.[4] The person has to be located in the same ontology. It is not always clear in just what way (a) my moving my arm or (b) my repaying a debt or telling the truth differ from (c) my arm moved or (d) a debt was repaid, a truth told. A further distinction is needed. With (a), there are two events:

(1) An arm (my arm) moved.
(2) I moved my arm.

With (b), there are three events:

(1) A debt was repaid, a truth was told.
(2) I repaid a debt, etc.
(3) Specific bodily events also occurred.

When I move my arm, my arm moves. Two events or one? How is *my moving* my arm an *event*? I cannot just move, I must move something, an arm, a leg, my mouth. Trying to move my arm when the muscles are cramped or perhaps temporarily paralyzed, is not something that can be witnessed, it is not a spatio-temporal event. So is my moving my arm a spatio-temporal event? The arm moving certainly is. We can easily determine when my arm moved because I moved it, as opposed to an odd muscle spasm or nervous tick. So there is a difference between (a1) and (a2). Thus, two events, even though we may find it difficult to describe (a2), *my moving* my arm, apart from the movement of the arm. Similarly with (b1) and (b2), a debt was repaid and I repaid the debt. In this case, of course, we can identify the method I used in repaying the debt: by check, credit card, or simply by handing the money to you. *How* I repaid you is not quite the same as *my repaying* you. But debts do not get repaid without someone doing the repaying (or someone arranging for automatic repayment by a machine at a certain date). So in this case, and with moral actions, a person is always involved. Nevertheless, we can record in our ledger that the debt was repaid *and* that Jones repaid it, he was the person who transmitted the money.

---

[3] *Subjects of Experience* (1996), pp. 140–6.
[4] As the quotation at the head of this chapter shows, Locke called attention to this distinction. For a discussion of Locke on action and the person, see my *Locke and the Compass of Human Understanding*, ch. 6. For other writers in the seventeenth and eighteenth centuries who also developed views on action, see my *Thinking Matter*, ch. 7.

Just how we count events may be open to some dispute, but what is important is to recognize that repaying a debt or telling the truth is not just the event of a debt repaid, a truth told: it is also the event of my repaying, my telling. In the same way, my moving my arm is not just the event of my arm moving; it is also *my moving* it. The ontological or metaphysical inventory is not yet complete. Besides (a1), an arm movement, and (b3), bodily events involved in repaying debts, bidding at auction, or telling the truth, there are events or processes in the brain, in the neurophysiology of the person. We need also to count events in perception. When I see the roses in my garden, my seeing is one event, brain processes are another series of events, and the processes from the surfaces of roses to sense organs are other events still. Depending on how we analyze my seeing roses, we will have to add other items, perhaps appearances, ideas or qualia to our inventory. Just as (a2) and (b1) require a person, so seeing roses requires a perceiver. The person is both actor and perceiver.[5]

II

The concept of the person developed by Locke and Kant, their ontology of the person, helps us locate the person and actions as well as appearances and qualia in our ontology. Locke's distinction between the person and the man is an example of the way a person as actor (mainly as a moral actor) is not identical with the man, the biological organism. The locus of responsibility is with the person, it is the person who acts, but of course the person is able to act because he has a body which is under his control. Locke makes this distinction between man and person mainly to highlight the importance of moral action (b1 and b2), although nonmoral actions (a1 and a2) also involve the man and the person. E. J. Lowe's account of Locke on the person tends to overlook the centrality in Locke's account of the moral dimension; instead he stresses Locke's remark that a person is a thinking, intelligent being with reason and reflection (*Essay* 2.27.9).[6] Lowe only briefly mentions the passages that talk of being *concerned* for the actions and for the ultimate rewards and punishments. The final summary given by Locke needs to be stressed:

---

[5] Cf. E. J. Lowe, *Subjects of Experience*, p. 140: "Persons or selves do not merely *perceive* their world – they also *act* upon it. Indeed, the self's capacities for perception and action are inseparably intertwined, even if these capacities may be exercised independently on some occasion."

[6] "Thus, the defining characteristics of personhood, for Locke, are rationality and consciousness, including *self-consciousness*." *Locke On Human Understanding*, p. 103; cf. p. 114.

the term person "is a Forensic Term appropriating Actions and their Merit; and so belongs only to intelligent Agents capable of a law, and Happiness and Misery" (*Essay* 2.27.26). That section continues with more talk of concern, happiness and rewards. It is this aspect of the person that Locke considered most important.

Lowe points out that some recent writers (he mentions Derek Parfit) offer a view adapted from Locke but different in some respects. That view, which Lowe labels the neo-Lockean view, considers person to be a construct of mental states.[7] Lowe quite properly stresses the constituting of persons: how "are persons supposed to be constituted by mental states."[8] He understands that Locke was interested in what *makes* a person be a person.[9] However, he does seem to suggest that Locke was interested in the criterion question: "Does Locke's definition of 'person' help him in his quest for a criterion of personal identity?"[10] Locke was not, I think, questing for a criterion; at least that was not his main concern. But criteria questions naturally arise from his concept of personal identity.

Locke was offering an account of what it is to *be* a person. To be a person is to be conscious of one's actions, to accept responsibility for them. Remembering what I have done is only one way of being conscious of them, although I do not suppose I can be conscious of my past actions and take responsibility for them, if I do not recall having done them. I am also conscious of present actions, concerned for them and accept responsibility for what I do. Rather than mental states, Locke's person might better be said to consist of actions, but this is misleading also. If we follow Locke's explication through the sections of *Essay* 2.27, we can gain some understanding of the nature of Locke's person or self. Of more importance is the relation between the self and its actions. Here is a summary of those sections:

Section 9: Person is an intelligent being with reason and reflection, "and can consider it self as it self, the same thinking thing . . ." The "considering" is done by consciousness. When we see, hear, etc., we know that we see, hear, etc. "and by this [knowing, awareness] every one is to himself, that which he calls self." He also distinguishes between himself and other *thinking things*. Note, too, the mention of reflection, another form of consciousness.

---

[7] *Subjects of Experience*, p. 23.   [8] *Ibid.*, p. 23.   [9] *Locke on Human Understanding*, p. 103.
[10] *Ibid.*, p. 104; cf. p. 105.

Section 10: Sameness of consciousness "makes a Man be himself to himself." Locke also speaks of the *personal self* and the consciousness he has of his present thoughts and actions: that consciousness makes the personal self *"its self* to it *self."*[11]

Section 11: Speaks of the personal self again and of the concern for its body.

Section 13: Reference to the individual *agent*, and to happiness and misery, rewards and punishments.

Section 14: One of the puzzle cases: he is no more one self with Nestor, etc. The "he" is the self because of being aware of specific actions, not the actions of Nestor. Should he find himself conscious of any of the actions of Nestor, he then would find himself to be the same person with Nestor.[12]

Section 16: "Had I the same consciousness, that I saw the ark," I would be the same self as Noah at the flood. Locke also speaks of concern and being accountable, also self consciousness (consciousness of self).

Section 17: Self = conscious thing "whatever substance made up of." The self is said to *own* its actions. In this passage, the "thing" seems to be different from the "substance." The phrase "intelligent being" in section 9 also does not refer to the standard substances, material and immaterial.

Section 21: A reference to *Human Identity*, in contrast to *Personal Identity*. A third-person reference.

Section 24: The "consciousness whereby I am *self* to my *self."*

Section 26: Consciousness is that "whereby it [the self] becomes concerned and accountable, owns and imputes to it *self*, past

---

[11] Consciousness also plays a role in Hume's discussion of the person or self in Book II of the *Treatise*. For example, "'Tis evident, that the idea, or rather impression of ourselves is always intimately present with us, and that our consciousness gives us so lively a conception of our own person, that 'tis not possible to imagine, that any thing can in this particular go beyond it" (p. 317). The next page speaks of "the impression or consciousness of our own person." Later, we are told that "the immediate *object* of pride and humility is self or that identical person, of whose thoughts, actions, and sensations we are intimately conscious" (p. 329). A person is characterized as a "thinking being" (p. 367), or as "a creature endow'd with thought and consciousness" (p. 411; cf. *Enquiry Concerning Human Understanding*, p. 98). Earlier in Book II, he speaks of the "self, or that individual person, of whose actions and sentiments each of us is intimately conscious" (p. 286).

[12] Cf. Hume, *Enquiry concerning the Principles of Morals*, p. 234: "No force of imagination can convert us into another person, and make us fancy, that we, being that person, reap benefit from those valuable qualities, which belong to him. Or if it did, no celerity of imagination could immediately transport us back, into ourselves, and make us love and esteem the person, as different from us."

Actions, just upon the same ground, and for the same reason, that it does the present." He goes on to stress happiness, pleasure and pain. The word "impute" is important in designating the action of the self with respect to past actions.

I am the owner of my actions, of the actions I accept as mine, the actions for which I am accountable. The referent of the "I" is not entirely clear, especially if we are trying to locate that referent in the standard ontology of Locke's time, an ontology of substance, of two substances, material and immaterial. Locke rejected the charge made by one of his critics that he had eliminated substance from his account of the world. But Locke was at pains to show that we do not have any clear idea of substance, other than the vague idea of a subject of properties. What was important for him were the characteristics and properties, the actions and passions of the objects we experience. The idea an Englishman has of a swan, for example, is "white Colour, long Neck, red Beak, black Legs, and whole Feet, and all these of a certain size, with a power of swimming in the Water, and making a certain kind of Noise" (*Essay*, 2.23.14). These properties are thought of as "united in one common subject." In the same way, we collect together the various operations of "our own Minds, which we experiment daily in our selves, as Thinking, Understanding, Willing, Knowing, and Power of beginning Motion, *etc.*"(2.23.15). We think of these as coexisting in one substance which unifies those properties, but we really have no clear idea of that common subject of the properties. It was the coexisting qualities, not the supposed substance, that was discovered by experience and observation; they were the objects of investigation in the science of bodies. It is those same coexisting qualities that make up our world. Locke did accept the current theory of corpuscular matter as a useful hypothesis, but he was primarily interested in the observed qualities, actions and reactions of material objects. The corpuscular theory, a theory about unobservables, can be seen as his content for the idea of material substance.

There is no similar theory of unobservables for the content of immaterial spirit. In some passages, Locke's use of the word "thing," as in sections 2.27.9 and 17 cited above, or in other passages the term "Being" (intelligent Being, 2.27.10), suggests a concern to avoid talk of substance while presenting his account of man and person. He does, however, sometimes write "the same Thinking thing, i.e. the same substance," so it may not be clear whether he did dismiss spiritual (immaterial) substance from his account. What *is* clear is that the concept of consciousness fills the unifying role for the person: "The same consciousness uniting those distant Actions into the same *Person*, whatever Substances contributed to their Production" (2.27.10). Consciousness even unifies the particles of our bodies to the person or self (2.27.11), so in that way consciousness is the unifier of mind and body. With consciousness playing the functional role of spiritual substance, Locke provides us with an experiential subject for the properties, abilities and actions of the complex, man and person. Since it is consciousness which makes or constitutes the person, we can say it is the person who unifies all those features. Person becomes a kind of substance, hence the phrase "thinking thing."

Lowe reaches a somewhat similar conclusion, first suggesting that the person for Locke has "the ontological status of (highly complex) *modes*," remarking that a mode is a quality or property of a substance.[13] On Lowe's account of Locke, the modes are "my own conscious mental history."[14] Perhaps the referent of "my" is the substance in the ontology Lowe believes Locke is accepting. But Lowe seems ambivalent, sometimes identifying the person with modes, at other times with the substance as "an *insubstantial* thing."[15] Is the person or self insubstantial because that self is not a substance, but modes of a substance? Or does its insubstantiality refer to the modes being mental? While presenting what he characterizes as a "neo-Lockean" view in his *Subjects of Experience*, Lowe explains that a mode is "any concrete non-substantial individual, or any entity wholly constituted by concrete non-substantial individuals" (p. 22). Examples are events, processes and states. This neo-Lockean view of persons says that persons are "wholly constituted by *psychological* or *mental* events, processes and states" (*ibid.*) Actions are not mentioned as part of that neo-Lockean account. Lowe does not, I think, agree with that account, although he recognizes that mental states do play some part in the constituting of persons. Lowe identifies the person with the substance: "a person or subject of mental states must be regarded as a *substance* of which those states are modes" (p. 32). That substance is a *psychological* substance, "a wholly distinctive kind of being" (p. 35). Such a substance on Locke's account, is neither material nor immaterial, but it can have both physical and mental properties.

---

[13] *Locke on Human Understanding*, p. 114.   [14] *Ibid.*   [15] *Ibid.*, p. 115.

Lowe's development of this concept of a psychological substance makes it an attractive addendum to Locke's analysis of the person. Whether Locke would have welcomed such an extension of his concept, whether he felt the need to place the person in an ontological category, is uncertain. There is, however, one interesting remark Locke makes while discussing the idea of space that may be relevant here. The question was, are space and body the same?

> Those who contend that *Space and Body* are *the same*, bring this *Dilemma*. Either this *Space* is something or nothing; if nothing be between two Bodies, they must necessarily touch; if it be allowed to be something, they ask, whether it be Body or Spirit? To which I answer by another Question, Who told them, that there was, or could be nothing, but solid Beings, which could not think; and thinking Beings that were not extended? (*Essay*, 2.13.16)

This passage might be seen as leaving open the possibility of a different ontological category for space. This passage could also be seen as showing Locke's indifference to ontological or metaphysical categories. There is one other place where he reveals such indifference or distrust of the standard ontology. This passage comes in a response to John Norris's question about ideas: are they modes or substances, material or spiritual? Locke replies: "If you once mention ideas you must be presently called to an account *what kind of thing you make these same ideas to be* though perhaps you have no design to consider them any further than as the immediate objects of perception."[16]

Perhaps Locke only wanted to consider the person as the subject or owner of actions. From the sections of *Essay* 2.27 listed above, it is clear that the person is not identified with the actions or thoughts, although the actions (and the considering, reflecting, imputing and the awareness of those actions or thoughts) do constitute the person, characterizing him and differentiating him from other persons. Locke can even say as he does in *Two Treatises* that "every Man has a *Property* in his own Person," or man is "Master of himself" and "*Proprietor of his own Person*."[17] It is his person which "any one unites" with the commonwealth.[18] Property is also explained as being that which men have in their person and goods.[19] Those repeated phrases in the *Essay*, "I am my self to my self," tell us

---

[16] "Locke's First Reply to John Norris," ed. Richard Acworth, *The Locke Newsletter* 2 (1971), 10.
[17] *Two Treatises of Government*, ed. Peter Laslett, Second Treatise, sections 27, 44.
[18] *Ibid.*, section 120.   [19] *Ibid.*, section 173.

how *I* acquire my *person*, how it becomes my property: by being conscious of my actions, taking responsibility for them, imputing them to myself, being concerned for happiness and eternal rewards. I am a man and I can become a person. Then I am both a man and a person. The "I" eludes any further analysis; Locke did not apparently think it needed any further analysis.

Locke does not provide us with any detailed analysis of the relation between the person and the man. He does consider the question of how we should treat the case of actions performed by a man while drunk, actions which, when he is sober, he does not remember or acknowledge. What this brief example reveals is that actions are performed by the man with his body. Body motion is one ingredient in actions. Body motion alone does not constitute actions such as bidding at auction, telling the truth, repaying a debt. For these, we need Locke's person with the knowledge and intention, concern and sense of responsibility, and perhaps as the head quotations to this chapter say, a reference to a rule or concept.

IV

In drawing a distinction between man and person, and in locating the source of human action, especially moral action, with the person, Locke could be seen as anticipating Kant's distinction between an empirical and an intelligible realm. Or Kant can be viewed as elaborating the details, both epistemological and ontological, of Locke's (or a Locke-type) distinction. All action involves the body, actions take place in the empirical domain. As such, they are subject to the laws of physics. They also take their place in a chain of causes where each event is determined by some prior event or events. The body motions involved in repaying a debt, telling the truth, or bidding at auction do not by themselves characterize or constitute those actions. On Locke's account the person is responsible for those actions, not directly for the body motions. Such responsibility (and intentionality) on the part of the person requires abilities and powers, both cognitive and ontic, in order to initiate those actions, to insert them into the world.

We become aware of our abilities and faculties by using them, by perceiving and acting. We are aware of them without observation or by introspection (Kant says "apperception"). However we characterize our knowledge and awareness of our abilities to make decisions and act upon them, such knowledge is not obtained in the way in which we

discover events in the physical world. The contrast between self-knowl-
edge and knowledge of events identifies two areas, two domains, two
aspects. In Kant's terminology, these are the empirical and the intelligible domains or aspects. This distinction does not mark a dualism in the
traditional sense; in fact, it constitutes a unity. Man is for Kant both a
phenomenon in the world with an empirical character, and an intelligible object with an intelligible character.[20] As a phenomenon, as an
object in the physical world of the body, man is of course subject to the
laws of physics and to the causality of events, natural causality. The
question arises, "can there be another kind of causality to account for
man as the agent of action?" Kant turns this question into an antinomy.
What is most useful about his statement and discussion of this question
is the explanation of the nature of agent causality, were there such a causality. If there is such a causality, it would be the cause of certain events
in the world. More specifically, such a cause would be "a power of absolutely beginning a state, and therefore also of beginning a series of consequences of that state."[21] The notion of "absolutely beginning" means
that there is no prior cause for the act of initiating some new event in
nature.[22] Absolute spontaneity of some action is necessary for imputing
that action to an agent.[23] Such an agent starts a new series of events, the
results, e.g., of a bid at a book auction. My decision to make a bid and
my *act* of bidding are not themselves part of the "succession of purely
natural effects, and are not a mere continuation of them."[24] That act
does "follow upon" prior events in the world but it does not "arise out
of" them, an important distinction drawn by Kant. Such is what the
thesis of the third antinomy lays before us.

Kant's sympathies are clearly with this thesis, despite its obvious
conflict with his insistence on universal causality, where each event is
fixed in a chain of natural causes. In the end, of course, Kant finds a
way of having both kinds of causality, at least, a way in which we can

---

[20] McDowell, whose analysis of Kant on action and agency is for the most part incisive, tends to
think Kant's appeal to the intelligible character removes the agent from the world: "Kant's
insight would be able to take satisfactory shape only if he could accommodate the fact that a
thinking and intending subject is a living animal"(*Mind and World*, Cambridge, Mass.: Harvard
University Press, 1996, p. 104). I am suggesting that Kant does depict the person as a "living and
intending subject" embedded in the world. McDowell offers a sensitive account of how actions
take place in the empirical world, an account very close to that offered by Kant (see pp. 70–80).
I discuss McDowell's important book in the Conclusion. He combines an account of agency in
and knowledge of the world which has a number of similarities to the account I find developing
in modern philosophy from Descartes to Kant.
[21] *Critique of Pure Reason*, trans by N. K. Smith (London: Macmillan, 1950), p. 409.
[22] *Ibid.*, p. 410.   [23] *Ibid.*, p. 412.   [24] *Ibid.*, p. 414.

accept the notion of absolute beginnings of events. His motivation for defending this thesis is two-fold: a commitment to moral responsibility and a metaphysical compulsion to find a way, at least a conceptual way, to break out of the tight causal chains of events in nature. For me to be responsible for my actions, I need to be free from the constraints of the laws of nature, but not free from moral laws which guide my decisions and my actions: two laws and two causalities. Under this concept the absolute beginning which I initiate gives me that freedom under the moral law.

The moral motivation driving Kant's discussion and resolution of the third antinomy was very strong; it is also well known. What has been given less attention is the metaphysical motivation, the motivation for allowing for first beginnings. This metaphysical concern links the third with the fourth antinomy. The link I see between these two antinomies does not concern, at least not directly or initially, the notion of an absolutely necessary being, as the fourth antinomy discusses. Rather, the interesting relation between these two antinomies revolves around the nature of an empirical series as *the conditioned*, and the corresponding concept of an *unconditioned beginning* of such a series. The thesis of the fourth antinomy asserts that "every condition [e.g., any empirical series of events] that is given, presupposes, in respect of its existence, a complete series of conditions up to the unconditioned which alone is absolutely necessary."[25] The thesis goes on to say that the necessary existence belongs to the sensible world; but therein lies the conflict raised by the thesis, since an absolutely necessary being cannot be part of the time series of sensible events. The notion of such a being clashes with the empirical series of events, each causally determined by prior events. But if such a being is to have an effect in the world, it must belong to the world: the very problem of the person as agent. Kant offers two possibilities: either the absolutely necessary being is the whole series of events itself or some part of that series.[26]

The antithesis of the fourth antinomy raises the question of the kind of causality such a necessary being would have. If that being belongs to the sensible world, its causality would also belong to that world, and hence it would not be an absolute beginning of the series. In terms of the third antinomy, each of us as an agent of our actions is an absolutely unconditioned cause of the actions we perform; at least, on the conception developed in that antinomy, we as agents of actions introduce new

[25] *Ibid.*, p. 416, B481.   [26] *Ibid.*, p. 417.

series into the world, each series begins with us.[27] The problem then
becomes to understand how this is possible, at least to find a way of conceiving its possibility, without introducing a dichotomy between the
agent as cause and the events that follow from agent causality and then
become subject to physical laws.

Two similarities to Locke are present in Kant's analysis. (1) The "I" in
every act of thought, and I would want to say in every action, especially
moral action, is not a substance; at least, it is not what we are conscious
of in acting and thinking: we are not aware of a substantial self.[28] (2) The
need for an unconditioned beginning of actions in the world, the need
for an intelligible cause, arises from moral considerations: the need for
freedom from the constraints on the initiation of actions, of natural causality. Kant does not explicitly extend the analysis in the fourth antinomy
to the self of moral action or to each empirical series of actions in the
world, but such an extension would seem to be implied in his account of
the third antinomy. One nagging question applies to both Locke and
Kant. In Locke's case, how are we to understand the relation between
man and person? In the case of Kant, how are we to understand the
relation between the empirical and the intelligible characters? Both
writers were trying to find a way of characterizing what Descartes
described as the unity of his two substances, a unity which Descartes saw
as a new category but for which he may have lacked a name.[29] Substance
talk is missing from Locke's account of the person and from that of
Kant, but it is one "entity," one item among many others in the physical, empirical world. That one item is able to initiate and take responsibility for actions that take their place in that very world.

One item ("entity") with two functions governed by two laws, moral
laws and physical laws, the latter for Kant being necessary laws. The
danger is that the empirical world threatens to engulf and consume the
intelligible functions. Kant was cautious about making dogmatic claims
for the reality of both domains, both functions; hence he resorted to

---

[27] Cf. Hume's definition of will: "by the *will*, I mean nothing but, *the internal impression we feel and are
conscious of, when we knowingly give rise to any new motion of our body, or new perception of our mind*" (*Treatise*,
p. 399).

[28] Kant, *Critique*, p. 319. Cf. Hume in Book 1 of the *Treatise*. What we are aware of on Locke's
account are the actions we have performed, the intentions we have had. The psychological substance suggested by Lowe, or the person as unifier and subject of those actions, is not a substance
in the sense of that term commonly understood in the seventeenth and eighteenth centuries.
Functionality has replaced substantiality.

[29] David Behan has suggested to me that the notion of an "incomplete substance," which Descartes
uses in some places, would cover this unity.

antinomies which present the pros and cons for the possibility and impossibility of both, of empirical, universal, necessary causes or of freedom, responsibility and unconditioned acts of free causality. The difficulty of defending the thesis side of the two antinomies highlights the ease that subsequent writers have found for discounting the duality of empirical and intelligible, of mental and physical. The attraction for making the body with its physical mechanism central, for trying to find in the complexity of neural networks all the explication needed of mental phenomena, becomes powerful. From explication to reduction becomes easy, naturalism and materialism result.

v

Just as actions ride on the backs of body motion, and just as persons are linked with but different from man (on Locke's account), so appearances (perceptions) are linked with brain events but are quite different in kind. As perceivers, we do not quite create appearances, although they are dependent on us in part. The brain can only create physical motion (electrical/chemical), perceivers can be said to create appearances when brain events of a specific sort occur. To say those events cause perceptions is misleading. Brain events can only cause physical events or, if we resist the notion of a noncausal interaction between perceivers and objects, we must say something about the kind of causation that has neural events causing awareness, sense qualia or appearances. Descartes's intriguing suggestion of brain motions serving as signs is one way to begin to detail a second kind of interaction. Brain events on this view function as signs to a conscious perceiver. We can then compare perceiving to understanding a language through the sounds and shapes of letters. Just as words are not physical, although closely related to and dependent on the sounds and shapes, so perceptions are psychological but dependent upon physical processes in the brain and nervous system.

When I see or look at a tree, the tree gets transformed from a physical, spatial object into a psychological object. In this way, the appearance of the object *is* the tree. Persons, actions and appearances share a domain. The person *is* the man, actions *are* body motions, appearances *are* the objects. In each case, something is added: to the man, a morally responsible person; to the body motion, an intentional, rule-following action; and to the independent object, a conscious awareness or mental content, an appearance.

It is time now to examine three specific writers, Locke, Berkeley and Hume, who treated the appearances, to use a phrase of Hume, as "the very things themselves" (chapters 4, 5, 6 and 7). At the end of those chapters, we will be ready to sketch a realism of appearances.

4
Locke on the knowledge of things themselves

> The idea is the cognitive response of the organism to the cognitive experience of a stimulus.
>
> John Deely, *New Beginnings: Early Modern Philosophy and Postmodern Thought*, p. 134

The main focus of the *Essay concerning Human Understanding* was on the nature and extent of our knowledge. What can we know? how much knowledge do we have? what kinds of items can be known? what are the areas of knowledge? These are some of the guiding questions for Locke. The final chapter of the *Essay* classifies the areas in which knowledge may be possible as the nature, properties and relations of things, the principles that should guide our moral actions, and the function of words and ideas in the pursuit of knowledge. Perhaps this third division of what he classifies as "the sciences" is the knowledge of knowledge. That may be what the doctrine of signs yields.

In the body of the *Essay* itself (and in other works by Locke), we find him exploring the nature and limits of what can be known, including God, bodies or external objects and their properties, the self and personal identity, liberty and necessity, causation and power, religious doctrines and dogmas. Knowledge is defined as our awareness or apprehension (Locke writes "perception") of the relation of ideas, ideas as signs. So ideas and the other sort of signs, words, function to produce knowledge in conjunction with the operations of the mind. Locke's reference to the doctrine of signs may be an inheritance from scholastic writings where there was such a doctrine, well-developed and extensively used.[1] One of the bothersome questions about Locke's talk of ideas as

---

[1] See John Deely, *New Beginnings: Early Modern Philosophy and Postmodern Thought* (Toronto: University of Toronto Press, 1994) and especially Robert Pasnau, *Theories of Cognition in the Later Middle Ages* (Cambridge: Cambridge University Press, 1997). Deely calls attention to the concluding section of the *Essay*, where Locke gave a division of the sciences, the doctrine of signs being the third of those sciences. Deely sees this passage in the *Essay* (a passage which C. S. Peirce took up later) as

signs, and his remark that idea-signs are the immediate object of knowledge, is "can we say we know bodies directly?" The question of direct
realism arises for us, if not for Locke.

The topic of realism may not have been one that Locke considered,
but there has been a long history of interpreting Locke as working with
a representative theory of perception and knowledge. The usual understanding of that theory is that ideas as signs represent the objects which
we claim to know. Idea-signs have been taken to be not only the represen-
tatives of objects, but the objects first known. From those idea-signs, on
this reading, we are either barred from knowing external objects (thus, we
are isolated in a realm of mental contents), or Locke is faced with finding
some way of deriving a knowledge of objects from an analysis of ideas
(thus, indirect realism at best). On this interpretation, idea-signs differ
from word-signs. We do not, I think, believe that in hearing or seeing
words, it is the words themselves that we know. Word-signs function as the
bearers of the meaning of the sounds or shapes. When we describe a rose
or a tree with words, the words direct our attention to what is described,
not to the describing words. Using Locke's terminology, we might try to
draw a parallel between word-signs and idea-signs by saying that words
are the immediate objects of the mind when we speak or write; but the
term "immediate" in this use does not turn word-signs into objects of
knowledge. Why do we take the term "immediate" when applied to idea-
signs as turning those signs into the objects of knowledge?

The status, nature and function of ideas in Locke's account of perception and knowledge has of course been the subject of much debate
over the years. I have offered various suggestions for reading Locke's
account as not making ideas stand between perceivers and external
objects. I do not want to open that topic again, but there are two related
issues which may have some bearing on the debate over ideas and the
question of realism in Locke. The first issue or topic is the nature of the
objects to which ideas refer. The second concerns Deely's discussion of
Locke's suggestion of a doctrine of signs.

Footnote 1 (*cont.*)

    a reflection, unknowingly, of some late scholastic doctrines, especially the work of John Poinsot
    (John of St. Thomas), his *Tractatus de Signis*. "The doctrine of signs as Locke sketched it was, there-
    fore, all unwittingly, actually more than a bare proposal. It was at the same time a kind of arche-
    typically unconscious summary of developments of the recent past achieved in the Iberian Latin
    world, and a harbinger of a contemporary development that would take place after Peirce" (*New
    Beginnings*, p. 140). Deely believes that Locke's suggestion about a doctrine of signs leads to a
    different concept of sign than is at work in the body of the *Essay*. I discuss Deely's distinction in
    section VI of this chapter.

I

There may be some uncertainty or ambiguity about the objects of knowledge in Locke's account, the objects which play a causal role in the generation of ideas. Are they the ordinary objects of everyday experience, the objects Locke often offers as examples, e.g., oyster, pineapple, clock, dogs, elephants, a lily, sugar, a rose, a violet, diamond, water, the Thames, ice, marble, globe of gold, a trumpet, hail-stones, snow, iron, an almond (just to cite a few)? These objects as such do not cause ideas; rather, it is some of their properties which are the causal agents, the powers of the bulk, figure and motion of their underlying corpuscular structure. Those corpuscles act on our sense organs and produce motion in nerves and brain. Locke does not explain just how ideas, mental contents, result from that causal process, but this much seems clear: it is the corpuscular structure of ordinary objects which acts on perceivers.

Locke talks about the objects we perceive, observe and experiment with in two ways. One way uses quality and phenomenological terms, referring to the color, shape, motion, etc., of ordinary objects, objects as a set of coexisting qualities. The other way is in terms of their corpuscular structure, a structure which is insensible. It is that structure which, in the theory Locke accepted, accounts for the action of objects on other objects and their effects on perceivers. Yasuhiko Tomida has recently offered a fascinating analysis of these two languages in Locke, two concepts of object, as it were.[2] Tomida refers to the first way of talking as talk about "experiential objects." The second way refers to "external objects" or to "things themselves."

when Locke distinguishes ideas from external things, what he thinks of as external objects are . . . minute particles that the corpuscular physics of his day took to be realities. (p. 60)

we can find two sorts of notion of body in the *Essay*. One is the notion used in the investigations of natural history. It is formed by extending our common-sense notion of body, and its archetype is what we ordinarily think of as a body. The other is the concept of "things themselves" as posited by the corpuscular hypothesis, and it is in several respects different from the ordinary notion. (p. 61; cf. p. 85)

Tomida has a very interesting account of how these two concepts of object are linked. It is not that linkage that I want to examine. Rather, I

---

[2] *Idea and Thing: The Deep Structure of Locke's Theory of Knowledge*, reprinted from *Annalecta Husserliana*, 46: 3–143 (Dordrecht: Kluwer Academic Publishers, 1995).

want to trace Locke's use of the phrase "things themselves" in the *Essay*, in order to determine if a case can be made for Tomida's claim that that phrase refers to the corpuscular structure of ordinary objects.

II

There are at least forty-three occurrences of the phrase "things themselves" in the *Essay*. They can be grouped under a few topics.

A. Look to experience, not to authority

(1) 1.4.23: His rejection of innate ideas. He has not followed authority, only truth. He suggests that progress in "rational and contemplative *Knowledge*" can be made if we seek it "in the Fountain, *in the consideration of Things Themselves*," and make use "rather of our own Thoughts than other Mens." Locke does not clarify the notion of "considering" things themselves. As other passages show, our access to things themselves is had via experience and observation. Consideration is offered in contrast with relying upon authority and other people's thoughts. Later passages speak of "contemplation" of things.

(2) 1.4.24: The same insistence here. Knowledge of universal truths results in "the minds of Men, from the being of things themselves, when duly considered"; these are "discovered by the application of those Faculties, that were fitted by Nature to receive and judge of them." He does not specify in this passage what the faculties are that are fitted to receive and judge of things. "Receive" probably refers to sensation, "judging" would be done by reason, reflection, comparing.

B. The sources of knowledge and the misuse of words

(3) 3.10.15: Refers to "unintelligible Discourses and Disputes, which have filled the Heads and Books of Philosophers" as examples of the abuse of words. He suggests that "we should have a great many fewer Disputes in the World, if Words were taken for what they are, the Signs of our *Ideas* only, and not for Things themselves."

(4) 3.11.5: The misuse of words can divert our attention from "the Fountains of Knowledge, which are in Things themselves."

(5) 4.5.4: We should avoid words such as "*Religion* and *Conscience*, of *Church* and *Faith*, of *Power* and *Right*, of *Obstructions* and *Humours*, *Melancholy* and *Choler*" and concentrate instead on the things themselves, i.e., what these terms refer to.

(6) 4.7.11: Maxims do not produce knowledge. Knowledge comes either from revelation or from "the things themselves." We "see the truth in them by perceiving their [ideas'] Agreement or Disagreement."

(7) 4.12.9: Since we lack a knowledge of the real essences, we can acquire knowledge by looking to the things themselves. "Here we take a quite contrary Course, the want of *Ideas* of their real *Essences* sends us from our own Thoughts, to the Things themselves, as they exist. *Experience here must teach me*, what Reason cannot: and 'tis by trying alone, that I can certainly know, what other Qualities coexist with those of my complex *Idea*."

(8) 4.16.6: On probability and assent. The "*highest degree of Probability*, is, when the general consent of all Men, in all Ages, as far as can be known, concurs with a Man's constant and never-failing Experience in like cases, to confirm the Truth of any particular matter of fact attested by fair Witnesses." He cites examples: "all the stated Constitutions and Properties of Bodies, and the regular proceedings of Causes and Effects in the ordinary course of Nature." Locke identifies this way of proceeding as an "Argument from the nature of Things themselves. For what our own and other Men's constant Observation has found always to be after the same manner, that we with reason conclude to be the Effects of steady and regular Causes."

(9) 4.17.22: Truth comes from "Proofs, and Arguments, and Light arises from the nature of Things themselves, and not from any Shame-facedness, Ignorance, or Error."[3]

(10) 4.21.5: Contemplation of the things themselves can lead to truth. The term "contemplation" may sound a bit odd to our ears in this context. It is a term which occurs frequently in the *Essay*. In the

---

[3] "Clownish shame-fac'dness" is described in Locke's *Some Thoughts concerning Education*, Section 142: "There is often in People, especially Children, a clownish shame-fac'dness before strangers, or those above them: They are confounded in their Thoughts, Words, and Looks, and so lose themselves in that confusion, as not to be able to do any thing or at least not to do with that freedom and gracefulness, which pleases, and makes them acceptable. The only cure for this, as for any other Miscarriage, is by use to introduce the contrary Habit."

chapter on Retention, Locke identifies contemplation as "keeping the *Idea*, which is brought into it [the mind], for some time actually in view" (2.10.1). We might say contemplation is the act of thinking about or even considering some idea or thought.

C. Relations of ideas to qualities of objects

(11) 2.2.1: Simple ideas: the "Qualities that affect our Senses are, in the things themselves, so united and blended, that there is no separation, no distance" between them, but ideas enter the mind singly.

(12) 2.8.8: He admits that sometimes he writes as if ideas were in "the things themselves," rather than in the mind. His example here is a snow-ball.

(13) 2.8.23: ". . . *real, Original*, or *Primary qualities*, . . . are in the things themselves, whether they are perceived or no." Secondary qualities depend upon the modifications of the primary. His examples are the sun, wax, fire, lead.

(14) 2.12.2: Simple ideas come from the things themselves, via sensation and reflection.

(15) 2.21.3 (In the long chapter on power.): Sensible qualities are powers of different bodies in relation to perception. When considered in the things themselves, they depend on the bulk, size, motion of the parts (i.e., the corpuscular structure of bodies).

(16) 2.21.55: ". . . pleasant Tastes depend not on the things themselves, but on their agreeableness to this or that particular Palate." Examples cited are cheese, lobsters, apples, plums, nuts.

D. Real, fantastical, true, etc., ideas

(17) 2.30.2: The ideas of whiteness, coldness or pain (as with snow) are not qualities of the snow, but the result of powers given to the object by God. They are, however, real ideas "whereby we distinguish the Qualities that are really in things themselves. For these several Appearances being designed to be the Marks, whereby we are to know, and distinguish Things, which we have to do with; our *Ideas* do as well serve us to that purpose, and are as real distinguishing Characters, whether they be only constant Effects, or else exact Resemblances of some thing in the things themselves."

(18) 2.31.8: Our abstract ideas of substances do not contain "all the simple *Ideas* [i.e. qualities] that are united in the Things them-

selves." We omit some of the qualities that we know "exist in" the object.

(19) 2.32.6: True and false ideas: to shorten the "way to Knowledge, and make each Perception the more comprehensive, the first Thing it [the mind] does, as the Foundation of the easier enlarging its Knowledge" is either "by Contemplation of the things themselves, that it would know; or conference with others about them, is to bind them into Bundles, and rank them so into sorts."

(20) 2.32.14: True and false ideas: we tend to take our simple ideas to be "in the Things themselves," but they are only marks God has given us to distinguish things.

(21) 3.3.11: General terms: universality "belongs not to things themselves, which are all of them particular in their Existence."

(22) 3.3.14: Men differ in the ideas they form of substances, even "where their abstract *Ideas* seem to be taken from the Things themselves, they are not constantly the same; no not in that Species, which is most familiar to us."

E. Substances

(23) 2.23.9: Qualities are powers in substances which produce ideas "in us by our Senses; which *Ideas* are not in the things themselves, otherwise than as any thing is in its Cause."

(24) 2.27.28: The difficulties that arise from the concepts of identity and sameness of substance or modes "arises from the Names ill used, [rather] than from any obscurity in things themselves. For whatever makes the specifick *Idea*, to which the name is applied if, that *Idea* be steadily kept to, the distinction of any thing into the same, and divers will easily be conceived, and there can arise no doubt about it."

(25) 2.32.18: ". . . our complex *Ideas of Substances, being all referred to Patterns in things themselves,* may be false." They are "all *false,* when looked upon as the Representations of the unknown Essences of Things." The term "pattern" is perhaps not as clear as it might be. I suggest that it at least refers to something we can observe or experience, perhaps the particular combination of qualities, the behavior of an object. See entry 35 below.

(26) 3.6.11: Our "*ranking,* and distinguishing natural *Substances into Species consists in the Nominal Essence* the Mind makes, and not in the real Essences to be found in the Things themselves." The term "found"

does not mean we can discover real essences, since Locke was firm on our knowledge being limited to observable coexisting qualities, i.e., to the nominal essence. So "found" means "this is where the real essence is located."

(27) 3.6.32: A similar point: ". . . several of those Qualities that are to be found in the Things themselves, are purposely left out of *generical Ideas*." The mind selects some qualities among those it finds coexisting together. In this passage, "found" does refer to what we can discover by experience and observation, i.e., coexisting qualities.

(28) 3.9.11: The signification of names: for substances, "we must follow Nature, suit our complex *Ideas* to real Existences, and regulate the signification of their names by the Things themselves, if we will have our names to be the signs of them, and stand for them."

(29) 3.11.24: Abuse of Words: with substances, "we are not always to rest in the ordinary complex *Idea*, commonly received as the signification of that Word, but must go a little farther, and enquire into the Nature and Properties of the Things themselves, and thereby perfect, as much as we can, our *Ideas* of their distinct Species; or else learn them from such as are used to that sort of Things, and are experienced in them. For since 'tis intended their Names should stand for such Collections of simple *Ideas* [qualities] as do really exist in Things themselves, as well as for the complex *Idea* in other Men's Minds, which in their ordinary acceptation they stand for; therefore to *define their Names right, natural History is to be enquired into*." Locke goes on in this passage to say that though men may speak properly "according to Grammar-Rules of that language, [they] do yet speak very improperly of Things themselves; and, by their arguing one with another, make but small progress in useful Truth and the Knowledge of Things."

(30) 4.4.11: The reality of knowledge: with substances, our ideas may fall short of being real since those complex ideas consist of "a Collection of simple *Ideas*, supposed taken from the Works of Nature, [they] may yet vary from them, by having more or different *Ideas* united in them, than are to be found united in the things themselves: From whence it comes to pass, that they may, and often do, fail of being exactly conformable to Things themselves."

(31) 4.8.10: Trifling propositions: Locke criticizes those who make the names of substances from their own ideas, rather than from "an Examination or Enquiry into the Nature of Things themselves."

F. Mixed modes

(32) 2.22.5: Locke asks the question of why we select just some qualities over others in forming mixed-mode ideas. We do so for our own purposes. But all the qualities "in the Nature of Things themselves, have as much an aptness to be combined and make distinct" ideas.

(33) 2.22.8: The names of mixed modes are a "fleeting and transient Combination of simple *Ideas*" which have only a short existence in the minds of men. He then gives an example: "For if we should enquire where the *Idea* of a *Triumph*, or *Apotheosis* exists, it is evident, they could neither of them exist altogether any where in the things themselves, being Actions that required time to their performance, and so could never all exist together."

(34) 2.22.9: One of three ways in which we can construct complex ideas of mixed modes is by experience and observation of things themselves. His example: "Thus by seeing two Men wrestle or fence, we get the *Idea* of wrestling or fencing."

(35) 3.5.12: Unlike the names of mixed modes, the ideas that the names horse or iron refer to are not considered "as barely in the Mind, but as in Things themselves, which afford the original Patterns of those *Ideas*."

(36) 3.9.7: What such words as "Murther" and "Sacrilege" signify "can never be known from Things themselves," since many aspects of such action words and ideas refer to the intention of the actor or to "the relation of holy Things."[4]

(37) 4.4.5: With mixed-mode ideas, the ideas are the archetypes for actions. Thus "we cannot but be infallibly certain," that all "the knowledge we attain concerning these *Ideas* is real, and reaches Things themselves." The phrase, "things themselves" here refers to the actions designated by our ideas.

(38) 4.4.9: If we make up our ideas of mixed modes, such as justice or temperance, will not relativism result, each person making those ideas to signify different actions or properties of actions? Locke's reply is that the actions of men have the properties that they have, no matter what words we use to name them. Here again the phrase, "things themselves" is used to refer to actions: there is no "confusion or disorder in the Things themselves."

---

[4] Cf. the head quote in chapter 3 on action words.

G. The limitations of knowledge

(39) 4.3.23: The ideas "we can attain to by our Faculties, are very dispro-
portionate to Things themselves."

(40) 4.3.28: We do not know or understand how thought could cause
motion in body or how body can cause thought in the mind. If
"Experience did not convince us, the Consideration of the Things
themselves would never be able, in the least, to discover to us" that
thought can act on bodies and bodies on the mind.

(41) 4.3.30: Where we lack knowledge, it may be due to "want of application in acquiring, examining" and comparing ideas together, not
"out of any imperfection of their Faculties, or uncertainty in the
Things themselves."

(42) 4.4.3: This is the passage which has often been noticed in debates
over the nature of ideas in his account. Locke asserts that "the Mind
knows not Things immediately, but only by the intervention of the
Ideas it has of them." He then raises the criterion question: "How
shall the Mind, when it perceives nothing but its own *Ideas*, know
that they agree with Things themselves?"

(43) 3.11.16: This is an interesting passage, not strictly for the limitation
of *knowledge*, as for the limitation of *demonstrative* knowledge. Locke
suggests that morality is capable of demonstration. Moral knowledge can be certain, the suggestion is, since in this case the things
themselves are the actions designated by our mixed-mode ideas.

III

What does the inventory of the occurrences of the phrase "things themselves" tell us about objects in Locke's account of perception and knowledge? Group A tells us that knowledge comes from our considering the
things themselves, rather than relying on authority or someone else's
claims. He urges us to use our own faculties in attending to the things
themselves. Group B underlines this general remark by commenting on
the way words can obscure our knowledge of things. Maxims are also
ruled out as a source of truth and knowledge. Example B7 speaks of
"looking to the things themselves," urging us to use experience in the discovery of knowledge. B8 is especially important for its account of the
argument from the nature of things themselves by using experience and
observation. B9 and 10 make similar points about truth.

Group C contrasts our ideas with the qualities of objects, and notes the difference between primary and secondary qualities. Ideas come from, are caused by, the things themselves. In fact, sensible qualities are said to be powers of the object, specifically powers of the primary qualities of the corpuscular structure of bodies. Group D continues along the same line, contrasting our ideas with the qualities and powers of the things themselves. Group E draws a similar contrast between our ideas of substances as a group of coexisting qualities and a supposed real essence (perhaps the corpuscular structure) of objects. We are limited to the groups of qualities we discover by experience and observation. Those qualities are, Locke says, "found in the Things themselves" (E27). E29 urges us to "enquire into the Nature and Properties of the Things themselves." The importance of natural history for such an experienced-based enquiry is also stressed. E31 again speaks of "an Examination of or Enquiry into the Nature of Things themselves."

Group F mainly makes the point that our ideas of mixed modes are not usually taken from things themselves, since they are features of actions which we form into action-names. F34 does indicate that sometimes our ideas of mixed modes can be taken from things themselves, e.g., by observing wrestling or fencing. F35 remarks that the names of objects such as iron and horse do refer to "patterns" in things themselves. F37 and 38 use the phrase "things themselves" to refer to actions, not to objects. Group G is concerned with the limits of knowledge, but G40 stresses the importance of experience in showing us that bodies do affect thoughts and thoughts can act on bodies.

If we set aside Group F as not relevant to the question of the referents of "things themselves" when dealing with physical objects (the referents for mixed-mode ideas are actions), it is clear that Locke uses that phrase to refer to what can be observed. From our observations, we form ideas of objects as groups of qualities and we can discover the uniformity of nature. That phrase does also refer to the corpuscular structure where the causation of sensory ideas is located, but that structure is the structure of all physical objects. The corpuscular structure certainly differs from the sensible qualities of those objects. So Locke uses the phrase "things themselves" to refer both to the experienced and observable features of bodies and to their insensible structure.

The same conclusion emerges when we trace Locke's use of the phrase "external objects," the other phrase that Tomida suggests refers to the particles of the corpuscular structure. The occurrences of this phrase (there are at least seventeen of them in the *Essay*) fall into two groups. One group deals with the causation of sensation and sensible ideas. The other group speaks of the discovery of qualities in external objects. Typical of the first group (there are eleven of these) is *Essay* 1.2.1: "God has given Sight, and the Power to receive them [ideas of colors] by the Eyes, from external Objects." Or *Essay* 2.14.27 where he refers to ideas that are caused by external objects. Those objects have the power to excite ideas in us (2.32.14,16). The second group of occurrences of the phrase "external objects" has the senses "conversant about external Objects," insisting that "the Mind cannot but receive those *Ideas*, which are presented to them" (4.13.2). We are also said to "observe a likeness or unlikeness of sensible Qualities in two different external Objects" (2.8.25), and we can see and feel external objects and acquire the idea of extension (2.13.24).[5]

Locke also employs another phrase, "objects themselves" for much the same purposes, to speak of the powers of objects, the causation of ideas, and the sensible features of objects (*Essay* 2.8.10, 14, 25; 2.11.5; 2.29.2; 3.2.6; 3.4.11). Another phrase he occasionally used is "outward objects," for example, "impressions made on our senses by outward Objects" (2.1.23,24; see also 2.19.1 and 2.21.1).

IV

The general sense of the phrase "things themselves" in Locke's usage seems to be "the referent of our ideas or thoughts." This would explain his using that phrase to refer to actions (the referent of mixed-mode ideas) and to physical objects (the referent of our ideas of bodies and their qualities). We know that Locke worked with a concept of body (physical object, material substance) which has bodies having an insensible corpuscular structure and which made that structure (at least, the particles of that structure) have the power of affecting other such objects as well as perceivers. That part of the concept of body did not derive from experience and observation; it came from the theory then current and employed by many scientists of the day (e.g., Boyle, Newton). The experiential concept of bodies did come from experience and observation: it gives us Locke's coexisting qualities, which are, on his account, the referent of names and ideas. So it is the combination of theory and experience-based knowledge that yields the concept of physical objects as a union of nominal and real essence, of coexisting qualities and corpuscular structure. The phrase "things themselves" (and those other

---

[5] For other references to "external objects," see *Essay* 2.1.3–5; 2.2.2; 2.8.4,12; 2.12.1; 2.19.1; 4.2.14.

phrases, "external objects," "objects themselves," and "outward objects") refers to this combination which characterizes the ordinary objects with which Locke is concerned. Whether it be a bit of gold or lead, a snowball or the frozen river Thames, a horse or a flower, a football or a clock, these "things themselves" have the dual nature of sensible qualities and insensible particles. The power that moves objects, and causes sensations and ideas in perception, a power given by God, comes from the insensible structure, the corpuscles, which on this theory have bulk and extension and the property of motion. Sensible objects have those same and other primary qualities, as well as the secondary qualities. The possession of secondary qualities by an object is perceiver-dependent (or better, dependent on the perceiver as well as on the corpuscular structure). It is the perceiver-dependence of some of the qualities of objects which raises a problem for understanding the nature of objects and also for ascribing direct realism to Locke's account.

v

Recognizing that Locke uses the phrase "things themselves" (and the other three locutions noted above) to refer both to ordinary objects available to sense perception *and* to those objects' corpuscular structure (especially to the powers of that structure), and keeping in mind that sensory ideas play a cognitive role in our knowledge of external objects, we need to ask "what information do our ideas give us of those objects?" The answer is complicated by the distinction between primary and secondary qualities, because of their difference in status. It is important to remember that sensible objects have both kinds of qualities. Body is defined as "a thing that is extended, figured, and capable of motion" (2.23.3). We discover the primary qualities of bodies by our senses (2.23.9). We also discover that bodies have secondary qualities as well, but these qualities do not belong to bodies in the same way as the primary qualities do: they depend upon the powers of the corpuscular structure as well as on perceivers. The same is true for our *awareness* of primary qualities: they also affect perceivers because of the actions of corpuscles, the processes in nerves and brain, and perceptual awareness. In the case of primary qualities, however, the fact that their appearing to perceivers is due in part to the cognitive apparatus of perceivers does not make them perceiver-dependent. Their *presence to* perceivers is of course perceiver-dependent, but their *existence as* properties of objects is perceiver-independent.

Ideas of secondary qualities play a somewhat different role for us from the ideas of primary qualities. They enable us to distinguish and use objects for our needs and purposes (4.4.4). In 2.23.8, Locke identifies secondary qualities as the "characteristical Notes and Marks" which lead us to "form *Ideas* of them in our Minds, and distinguish them one from another." The ideas of secondary qualities play an important functional and operational role for us and for scientists, but they also inform us that objects have the powers to cause us to have those ideas, they "represent" or "answer to" those powers of objects (2.32.16).[6] The information carried by our ideas about the causal powers of corpuscles is not contained in ideas in the same way that the information, e.g., that gold is yellow, malleable, fusible, dissolvable in *aqua regia*, is contained there. The latter information is obtained by experience and observation. We watch what happens when we place a piece of gold in *aqua regia*, we test it for malleableness, and we can check the color. All of this just by looking. That information is stored in our idea of gold, the acquisition of that information precedes the acquisition of those ideas. When we look and observe, when we note and record what we see or feel, we do not do so by first having the ideas produced by the looking. Observing is not, as it were, looking through or with ideas, at least not the ideas we end up with after looking.

The information that those ideas are caused by corpuscular power is not contained in the ideas of yellow, malleable, etc.: it results from our accepting the corpuscular theory and from our concluding that there are causes for the appearances we experience and the ideas we acquire. How do our ideas contain the information that some qualities we observe are perceiver-dependent? Locke does cite (in 2.8) some evidence for the variability of secondary qualities and the fact that some primary qualities persist through change; but if these features are evidence for the distinction, that evidence requires some reasoning, some inferences. Thus, that information is not contained in the ideas of secondary qualities as such: it rests on our ideas of cause, power, and perhaps existence.

So the representation by ideas of the things themselves (1) spans the sensible and insensible aspects of objects, (2) combines ideas acquired by experience and observation with (3) reasoning and inference and (4) the corpuscular theory. We might want to say these features of our ideas add up to a representative theory of *knowledge*, where "represent" covers the

---

[6] For a full discussion of "representation" in Locke's use, see that entry in my *Locke Dictionary* (Oxford: Blackwell, 1993).

four kinds of information with their different sources of acquisition. To speak of a representative theory of *perception* is much more dubious.

VI

We would be hard-pressed to find in the above inventory of references to the things themselves material for or even hints at a representative theory of perception. Ideas are referred to in some of the entries, but the main stress is upon observation and experience, looking to the things themselves, considering them and their relation to our ideas and thoughts. What role do ideas as signs play in the collecting of information from the environment? What, in fact, has become of the notion of ideas as signs? Can we even say what Locke meant by ideas (along with words) being signs?

The bulk of Locke's talk of signs concerns words. Out of close to one hundred references to signs in the *Essay*, only four are about ideas. It is not, I believe, until 2.32.19 that we get a clear reference to ideas as signs. Discussing true and false ideas in that section, Locke says truth involves the joining or separating of signs, and the "signs we chiefly use, are either *Ideas* or Words, wherewith we make either mental, or verbal Propositions." Idea-signs are the components of mental propositions. The next reference to ideas as signs comes in his discussion of general terms. General and universal "concern only Signs, whether Words, or *Ideas*" (3.3.11). General ideas represent many particular things. He also speaks in that passage of the signification of words or ideas. No more talk of idea-signs until 4.5.2, where truth is defined as "*the joining or separating Signs, as the Things signified by them, do agree or disagree one with another.*" Signs are joined or separated in propositions. He repeats his remark about two kinds of proposition, mental and verbal, adding here: "as there are two sorts of Signs commonly made use of, *viz. Ideas* and Words." The final reference to idea-signs comes at the close of the *Essay*, the passage that interests John Deely, with the cryptic reference to a doctrine of signs and his use of (or coining of) the word "semeiotike." In that passage, "Logick" is said to be the consideration of "the Nature of Signs, the mind makes use of for the understanding of Things, or conveying its Knowledge to others" (4.21.4). Signs play a role in understanding and communicating. No mention of any role they play in perception, in looking, observing, testing. Locke continues with this oft-quoted remark: "For since the Things, the Mind contemplates, are none of them, besides it self, present to the Understanding, 'tis necessary that something else,

as a Sign or Representation of the thing it considers, should be present
to it: And these are *Ideas.*" Again, perception is not mentioned, it is "contemplation" and "considering" that employ ideas.

Deely considers that passage in *Essay* 4.21.4 as a proposal, not a
description of what Locke has done in the *Essay* itself. That proposal
involves, Deely believes, a different concept of sign than the one Locke
employs when he says ideas are signs. The concept of sign that Deely
contrasts with Locke's idea-signs (and which he thinks might be implicit
in the suggestion of a doctrine of signs) is of a sign that works silently in
making objects present to the mind. Those signs are not themselves
objects of the mind. Descartes's ideas can be viewed this way (in their
objective reality role); and some late scholastic writers – Poinsot about
whom Deely writes is one – employed that notion. Locke's ideas are
objects, Deely says, not signs of this sort. Locke does use the term
"object" when he explains that he uses "idea," as others have used
"species," "phantasm" or "notion" (1.1.8). Deely considers this notion of
idea as the objects of the mind "a common modern doctrine," a doctrine that is "distinctly modern" from Descartes and Locke to Kant.[7]
The "basic assumption at work [in these writers] is that the mind directly
knows only its own products" (p. 16).[8]

In a passage added to the fourth edition of the *Essay*, while explaining a change in terminology from "clear and distinct" to "determined
and determinate" ideas, Locke does speak of ideas "*which the Mind has in
it self, and knows.*"[9] That same passage speaks several times of ideas as
objects in the mind, articulate sounds are said to be the signs of determinate ideas. An idea in the mind is also characterized as "*a simple appearance,*" and the mind is said to have it "in its view" and it "perceives it in
its self."[10] Ideas are also said to be *present in* the mind, and an idea is
described as the *immediate object* of the mind. The mind perceives (that is,
is aware of), knows and sees the ideas that are present to it. The common
locution throughout the *Essay* is of ideas being *in the mind.*[11] The notion
of the mind "knowing" its ideas, is not, I think, Locke's usual way of
speaking about knowledge. He defines knowledge as the perception of

---

[7] Deely, *New Beginnings*, p. 110.
[8] Pasnau identifies two views about species in scholastic accounts, a naive and a sophisticated
theory. "On the naive account, species are themselves the objects of cognition . . . The naive
species theory rejects direct realism. It holds, instead, a representationalist theory of perception,
according to which it is species that we directly perceive, whereas the external world is perceived
indirectly" (*Theories of Cognition*, p. 195). For the sophisticated theory, "species may be intermediaries between our cognitive faculties and the external world, but they will be only causal intermediaries. Species will not themselves be the objects of cognition, because they play their role
at an entirely subcognitive level."   [9] Epistle to the Reader, p. 13.   [10] *Ibid.*, p. 14.
[11] For example, *Essay*, 2.31.4 and 3.2.4, 8.

the relations of and between ideas. He urges us to look to the things themselves, to rely upon experience and observation. We can say that *knowledge* (and probability) is a product of our actions. Ideas and the perception (awareness) of them are important ingredients in knowledge; they, and the relations of coexistence, identity and diversity, necessary connection, and real existence carry information about the world. Equally important for knowledge are experience and observation, the argument from experience. To say that what the mind knows directly are only the products of our minds seems to suggest that looking, feeling, moving objects are somehow indirect, that we must first have ideas and then look through them to the things themselves. Looking, sensing, observing, testing are of course actions we perform, actions involving physical and neurophysiological events as well as psychological states and processes. When Locke instructs us to try pressing a football between our hands as a way to acquire the idea of solidity, the feeling of resistance, our inability to bring our hands together will yield some understanding of solidity, along with impenetrability and resistance. The looking, the muscular feelings experienced, do not themselves involve ideas, we are not looking and feeling through or by means of ideas. The looking and feeling do involve psychological events, felt sensations, tactuo-muscular experiences. We would not, I think, say that because such psychological events constitute our awareness of the football, therefore we do not experience or know the football directly. The terms "directly" and "immediately" used by Locke were part of the seventeenth-century vocabulary employed to meet the principle that what is known must be present to the mind, a principle found in many writings of the seventeenth and eighteenth centuries.[12] They do not require that our knowledge of bodies, of physical objects, be indirect, the result of inference, mediated by mental modes.

In saying Locke's ideas are objects, objects directly known, Deely is in agreement with many readers of Locke. That interpretation has of late been challenged by other readers, myself included.[13] As I remarked

---

[12] On this curious notion of presence to the mind in the writings of the seventeenth and eighteenth centuries, see my *Perceptual Acquaintance*, chs. 3 and 4. Arnauld famously charged Malebranche with confusing physical presence with cognitive presence. The notion of presence occurs in a few places in Locke's *Essay*. It is relevant to remember that Locke followed the Malebranche–Arnauld exchange closely while he was in the final stages of the composition of the *Essay*. As I remarked above in chapter 1, that curious notion keeps reappearing even today.

[13] For a brief discussion, see my *Locke Dictionary*, the entry for "idea." Also my *Perceptual Acquaintance*, ch. 5. Among other considerations, it is worth noting that there are passages in the *Essay* that replace the talk of ideas as objects with the term "appearances." For example: "For our *Ideas* being nothing but bare Appearances or Perceptions in our Minds" (2.32.1; see also 2.32.3, 2.1.3, and 2.10.2).

earlier in this chapter, I do not want to rehearse my arguments for a different reading of Locke's ideas. What is worth our attention is Deely's discussion of the doctrine of signs in Poinsot and other late scholastics, especially his positioning Locke's proposal in the tradition prior to the *Essay*, although unbeknownst to Locke. To say, as Deely does, that the 4.21.4 proposal implies a concept of sign different from that assumed in the body of the *Essay*, suggests that we can find in the *Essay* an account of signs, words or ideas. I do not think there is much material in that book for saying how signs work, what the sign relation is.[14] Between words and ideas, that relation is one of "standing for," being "a name or mark of." Idea-signs are not described as marks for things, but Locke does say they correspond to things, their patterns are in the things, or ideas represent things. So I would agree, there is no doctrine of signs in the *Essay*, despite much talk of word-signs and a few references to idea-signs.

Can we say anything more definite about the concept of sign implied by the 4.21.4 suggestion of a doctrine of signs? I believe Deely thinks we can, based mainly on his identification of Locke's ideas as objects of the mind, objects which we know. Also, the fact that Locke used the term "semeiotic" in its Greek form,[15] together with C. S. Peirce's reference to Locke's proposal, reinforces Deely's conviction that in a kind of unconscious way, Locke's proposal echoes earlier and anticipates later developments in semiotics.

I do not think we can say with any certainty just what Locke had in mind in that final chapter. He does not tell us enough about what would be different in that "Logick and Critick." It is a tantalizing suggestion, coming at the end of the *Essay*, but it is difficult to determine whether Locke meant it to refer to the account of knowledge and understanding in the prior books of the *Essay*. That work was not itself a work of natural philosophy, the first of the three sciences listed there, but it does contain remarks about the "Constitutions, Properties, and Operations" of matter, body and spirits, as well as our knowledge of things, the concerns of natural philosophy he cites (4.21.1). The second of the three sciences, with ethics as the main component, receives much attention and analysis in the *Essay*. There are many remarks throughout that work on the importance of the "Right applying our own Powers and Actions, for the Attainment of Things good and useful," his characterization of

---

[14] I discuss this topic in my *Locke and the Compass of Human Understanding: A Selective Commentary on the Essay* (Cambridge: Cambridge University Press, 1970), ch. 9.

[15] For Deely's discussion of Locke's term, its possible source, see *New Beginnings*, pp. 111–13.

ethics (4.21.2). The third science Locke listed as the doctrine of signs seems to be one of the dominant concerns of the entire work, at least for word-signs and their relation to ideas. So why is this division of the sciences, of areas of knowledge or disciplines, not just a summary reminder of what Locke has done in the *Essay*, calling attention to the importance of paying close attention to the language we use, to the words and ideas we use, in order to avoid confusion and unclarity? Perhaps the last several sentences of this section can be viewed as sounding as if the *Essay* has not applied that different logic to "the whole Extent" of human knowledge. Perhaps Locke considered his *Essay* as only laying the groundwork for such a logic, leaving it to others to follow his lead and to apply the notion of word- and idea-signs to specific domains. One of the consequences of such an enterprise would be, Locke suggests, a different "Logick and Critick." There is a logic sketched in places in the *Essay*, an informal logic or a logic for use. He attacks the standard Aristotelian logic used in the university.[16] It is also interesting that Locke thought the art of criticism would be improved by a careful attention to words and ideas.[17]

If Deely's suggestion is accepted, that Locke's concluding remark about a doctrine of signs sets a different role for idea-signs than the one in the body of the *Essay*, the concept of representation in a doctrine of signs becomes more like Descartes's objective reality:

Within the family of notions covered by the term "idea" in Locke's sense of the intraorganismic factor enabling awareness of whatever objects we experience or know, it strikes me that two in particular are the most fundamental: *representatio* and *species*. "Representatio" is fundamental because it designates the fundamental function of every idea in making present within awareness objects regardless of their proximity within the environment. This is the main function of idea, certainly, that Locke had in mind [in his proposal?], as also Descartes . . . [18]

A representative theory of perception would then be one which has ideas making objects present to us. The objects would still be objects of experience, the objects that appear to us. Valuable as Deely's suggestion is, we do not have to place Locke's doctrine of signs between Poinsot and

---

[16] See my *Perceptual Acquaintance*, my *Locke and the Compass*, and especially my article, "Schoolmen, Logic and Philosophy," *The History of the University of Oxford*, vol. 5, ed. L. S. Sutherland and L. G. Mitchell (Oxford: Clarendon Press, 1986), ch. 20, pp. 565–91.

[17] Samuel Johnson, in his *Dictionary*, quotes that final sentence of *Essay*, 4.21.4 under the "science of criticism." See his entry for "Critick."

[18] Deely, *New Beginnings*, p. 126. I assume that in saying this is the function of ideas that Locke had in mind, Deely does not mean throughout the *Essay*, but only implicit in his proposal.

Peirce in order to see that ideas on Locke's account throughout the *Essay* are not intermediaries between perceivers and objects. Especially when we understand that some of our ideas are acquired by looking, observing and experimenting, it seems that experience and observation are not chained to, or trapped behind, the very ideas that arise from those activities. We look to the things themselves, as they appear to us in our experience, we acquire various ideas, we reflect and reason about those ideas and our experience, and we then derive the complex information by some analysis of or just by attending to our ideas.

VII

Deely's material on late scholastic sign theory is important for the background out of which modern philosophy and its concern with knowledge and perception arose. The sign theory in that tradition treats signs as *formal* signs; a formal sign is not itself an object of the mind but works to present objects to the mind. Descartes's objective reality fits in that tradition. His *being* of objects in the mind is clarified by Arnauld as epistemic. Berkeley's ideas become things in the same way. Hume uses the notion of presence in his discussion in Book I of the *Treatise*. Each of these writers reflects aspects of the scholastic–Cartesian account. Locke was not much interested in these notions of presence to the mind, of objects existing in the mind, but there are a number of echoes of those debates in his *Essay*. I would just cite a few. (1) His reference to species, phantasms, and notions as alternative terms for whatever it is the mind is aware of in perception. (2) The addition in the fourth edition of the *Essay* of the terminology of determined and determinate (for clear and distinct), with the explicit reference to the objective reality of ideas. (3) Even a reference, in that final section, to the notion of presence to the mind. (4) And I think we can include his talk of ideas as signs (along with words). None of these, of course, is used to present a theory of perception, none addresses the problem of how ideas arise in the mind. The details of these issues were left to one side by Locke. He was trying to address questions of perception without the details of these earlier theories. He believed his account of perception and knowledge was neutral between species, phantasms and notions.

5

The notions of Berkeley's philosophy

Notions govern mankind . . .

Alciphron, Dialogue 4

Pray tell me, are not speech and style instrumental to convey thoughts and notions, to beget knowledge, opinion and assent?

Alciphron, Dialogue 6

The title of this chapter is intentionally ambiguous. Usually we take the term "notion" to refer to Berkeley's characterization of the knowledge of spirit (soul, mind) and of God (and also of relations). That use of the term distinguishes it from the way we know physical objects, by sensation and perception. But the phrase "notions of" signals a more interesting use of "notion," to use one of the *OED* definitions, as "ideas, views, opinions, theories or beliefs," a use which the *OED* dates to 1603. Thus, the ideas, views, opinions, theories and beliefs found in Berkeley's writings, which he defended, would fit that definition. In fact, when we examine his various books and essays, the terms "notion" and "notions" occur frequently throughout. In the dialogue books, *Three Dialogues* and *Alciphron*, he employs these terms to refer to views of the different interlocutors in those exchanges. Theories or opinions or beliefs that one of the dialogue characters wishes to reject are labeled as disruptive, impious, evil and leading to skepticism or atheism. We also find many examples of specific notions; the terms are occasionally used interchangeably with "idea" or "impression."

Paying attention to an author's use of certain words or phrases can sometimes disclose aspects of his thought, or of the tradition behind his writings, not always noticed when we read and analyze his writings. Whether a careful inventory of the uses of the term "notions" in Berkeley's books will add to our understanding of his thought, whether it might even cast some light on the more radical features of his philosophy, are questions I wish to explore.

I

The term "notion" has had various specialized uses in modern philosophy. In some scholastic writers, it played the role of presenting objects to the perceiver, similar to what Descartes tried to achieve by the objective reality of ideas.[1] A contemporary of Locke, John Sergeant, tried to adapt the Cartesian objective reality of ideas for his own purposes, to make notions the objects as they exist in the mind (*Solid Philosophy Asserted*, 1697). Sergeant's notions were cognitive contents, meanings as he termed them. Other writers invoked notions as conceptual contents, in criticism of Locke's liberal use of "idea" as "whatever it is, which the Mind can be employ'd about in thinking" (*Essay*, 1.1.8).[2] A writer who stressed, as did Locke, experiment and observation as the method to science, criticized "the *notional Theorems* in philosophy," meaning theories not based on observation.[3] Culverwel characterized innate principles as "Alphabetical Notions."[4] Bishop Wilkins remarks that the construction of what he called a "real character" for language should be made "*from the Natural notions of things.*"[5]

There were more specialized, somewhat technical uses of the term. Locke had his own special use. The essences of what he calls "mixed modes" are, he says, "by a more particular Name called *Notions*; as by a peculiar Right, appertaining to the Understanding" (*Essay*, 3.5.12). He repeats this remark in one of his replies to the Bishop of Worcester: "the term 'notion' is more peculiarly appropriated to a certain sort of those objects, which I call mixed modes" (In *Works*, ii. 133). There is, however, no systematic use of this term when talking of mixed modes or human actions. But the term "notion" in Locke's *Essay* is more extensive than his special use to designate mixed modes.[6]

The appearance of this term in Locke's *Essay* covers many uses different from this special use for mixed modes. Sometimes "idea" and

---

[1] See Alexander Broadie's *Notion and Object: Aspects of Late Medieval Epistemology* (Oxford: Clarendon Press, 1989),1.
[2] See for example, Charles Mayne's *An Essay concerning Rational Notions* (1733) or the work usually assigned to a Zachary Mayne, *Two Dissertations concerning Sense and the Imagination* (1728).
[3] Maynwaring, *Praxis Medicorum Antiqua et Nova* (1671).
[4] Culverwel, *An Antidote Against Atheisme* (1655).   [5] Wilkins, *An Essay Towards a Real Character* (1668).
[6] The next two paragraphs have been adapted from the entry on "notions" in my *Locke Dictionary*.

"notion" are used interchangeably (e.g., 1.1.3; 2.14.5; 2.22.11). There are other references to "vulgar" or ordinary notions (2.31.2,12; 4.10.18). We also find many references to claims Locke believed to be false or worse: he calls them odd notions, 2.1.18 (that the soul always thinks); wrong notions influenced by custom (2.11.2; 2.21.69); people who use their words for unsteady and confused notions (2.33.9; 3.10.4); and the imperfect notions children have (3.11.24). Locke mentions a number of specific notions. He remarks that blind persons cannot have any notions of colors or deaf men of sounds (2.2.2), and his account of memory reminds us that after some years "there is no more Notion, nor Memory of Colours" (2.10.5). Substance is deemed an important notion (2.13.18); we are told what is required to have "true distinct Notions of the several sorts of Substances" (2.23.7), he refers to "this Notion of immaterial Spirit" (2.23.31), he speaks of the notions of gratitude and polygamy (2.28.9), of our notions of matter and thought (4.3.6), and even of a notion of God (4.8.6). When he discusses the claims for innate principles that involve God (e.g., that God is to be worshipped), he employs the term "notion" more frequently than the term "idea." Phrases such as "a notion of God," "the notion of a law-maker," "the notion of his maker," occur frequently in 1.4.8–15. When he deals with Herbert of Cherbury's account of common notions, principles or truths, the term "notion" replaces "idea" again (1.3.15; cf. 1.3.16,17).

There are also places in the *Essay* where Locke speaks of the origin and acquisition of notions. The innatist claimed that there are in the understanding "certain *innate Principles*; some primary Notions" (1.2.1). Locke of course rejected that claim, insisting that all ideas are acquired from sensation or reflection. Some acquired notions (he uses the Cartesian phrase, "adventitious Notions" in 1.2.25) can influence our perceptual judgments (2.9.8). The brief summary of his account of idea acquisition speaks of "the Originals of our Notions," seeming to suggest that those originals are ideas, that notions are derived from ideas (2.12.8), a suggestion that he explicitly applied to his analysis of causation: "the Notion of *Cause* and *Effect*, has its rise from *Ideas*, received by Sensation or Reflection" (2.26.2). The chapter on faith and reason asserts that simple ideas "are the Foundation, and sole Matter of all our Notions, and Knowledge" (4.18.3). The first chapter of Book III on language notes the link between ideas and words, but uses the term "notion" rather than "idea":

It may also lead us a little towards the Original of all our Notions and Knowledge, if we remark, how great a dependance our *Words* have on common sensible *Ideas*; and how those, which are made use of to stand for Actions and Notions quite removed from sense, *how their rise from thence, and from obvious sensible* Ideas *are transferred to more abstruse significations*, and made to stand for *Ideas* that come not under the cognizance of our senses; . . . (3.1.5)

He wonders in this same passage "what kind of Notions they were, and whence derived, which filled their Minds, who were the first Beginners of Languages."

II

The wide variety of uses of the term "notion" by Locke may reflect common modes of speech among writers.[7] The same variety, many of the same examples, are found in Berkeley's writings. I have surveyed his *Principles*, the *New Theory of Vision*, the *Three Dialogues*, *Alciphron*, and the essays in *The Guardian* credited to Berkeley. I have grouped the uses under categories or types.

(1) Notions held by Berkeley, or by particular persons in the dialogues

These appear as "my notions," "our notions," etc.
Principles, Preface: Refers to the "novelty and singularity" of some of his notions.

  Section 44: Refers to his notions of tangible objects.
  Section 48: Refers to Section 45 and the objection that on his notions ["our notions"], it does not follow that objects are annihilated when not perceived by us.
  Section 58: Refers to the notions "we advance."
  Section 134: Refers to people who have a prejudice against "our notions."

---

[7] The journal, *The Free-Thinker*, may reflect this general use. For example, essay no. 155 for September 14, 1719, speaks of "comparing all new Ideas (as they present themselves) not only one with another; but likewise, with Notions, it was before possessed of" (vol. 3, p. 241). For other uses of the word "notion" in this journal, see pp. 240, 242 (standard notions), 243 (general notions, notion of the antipodes). In essay no. 156 for September 15, 1719, p. 244 (approved and settled notions), pp. 245, 246, 247 (notion of government). This journal was started by Ambrose Philips (1675?-1749), a renowned essayist who contributed to *The Guardian*, the widely known eighteenth-century journal, engaged Alexander Pope in debates about writing poetry, and was active in other literary enterprises. *The Free-Thinker* ran from May 1718 to September 1719. Its subtitle reads: "or Essays on Ignorance, Superstition, Bigotry, Enthusiasm, Craft, &c. Intermix'd with several Pieces of Wit and Humour. Design'd To restore the Deluded Part of Mankind to the Use of Reason and Common Sense."

Dialogue One[8]

  p. 191: Hylas confesses that he does not know how to give up his old notions.

Dialogue Two

  p. 208: Hylas refers to the notions he was led into by Philonous.

  p. 220: Hylas now finds the notion of occasion groundless. He goes on to admit that he is now less fond of the notions he used to hold.

  p. 221: Philonous refers to Hylas's notions: he has shifted from one to another.

Dialogue Three

  p. 226: Hylas suspects all his former notions.

  p. 235: Philonous remarks that some heathens and philosophers affirmed the absolute existence of some beings independent of all minds, but notions that are consistent with the Bible deny this. Hylas asks Philonous what difference there is between real things and chimeras, on Philonous's notions.

  pp. 237–8: Philonous: What makes people averse to his notions is a belief that he denies the reality of sensible things. He offers two definitions of "matter," (1) insensible substance or (2) sensible bodies.

  p. 250: Hylas charges that the scriptural account of creation differs from Philonous's notions, irreconcilably in fact. Hylas repeats this charge in his next speech.

  p. 252: Philonous answers Hylas's charge by insisting that his notions are not incompatible with the Mosaic account. His account, in fact, fits "the common, natural, undebauched notions of mankind."

  p. 255: Philonous suggests that Hylas thinks there is no repugnancy between the received notions of materialists and the inspired writings.

  p. 256: Philonous: Those who accept matter destroy the sense of Moses, their notions are inconsistent with that account. He goes on to say that Hylas has to reconcile his notions to the account of creation. Hylas agrees with Philonous now, but he still feels a sort of backwardness towards Philonous's notions. Philonous suggests Hylas is just stuck in old and rooted notions.

  pp. 261–2: Philonous: At the end of a long speech, he suggests that the

---

[8] I use this way to refer to the *Three Dialogues Between Hylas ad Philonous* (*Works*, ed. A. A. Luce and T. E. Jessop, 9 vols., London: Nelson, 1948–57), indicating to which of the three the references belong.

difficulties they have just discussed apply to Hylas's own notions.
Hylas refers to his and Philonous's notions.

p. 262: Philonous says he has not set up new notions but has just combined two truths shared by the vulgar and philosophers: "the things
we immediately perceive are the real things" and "the things immediately perceived are things which exist only in the mind." He characterizes these as two notions.

Alciphron, Dialogue 1

Section 12: Alciphron speaks about the "spreading of our notions" (p.
31). He goes on to claim that "All our discoveries and notions are in
themselves true and certain; but they are at present known only to
the better sort" (p. 54). Euphranor is not surprised that "vulgar
minds should be startled at the notions of your philosophy."

Section 13: Alciphron refers to "general reflections on our notions" (p.
54).

Section 15: While they were discussing proofs for Alciphron's views,
Euphranor wants to know "whether the notions of your minute philosophy are worth proving" (p. 60).

Alciphron, Dialogue 2

Section 7: Euphranor to Lysicles: "hath not old England subsisted for
many ages without the help of your notions?" (p. 75)

Section 15: Lysicles: "This thing of dignity is an old worn-out notion,
which depends on other notions old, and stale, and worn out, such
as an immaterial spirit" (p. 87).

Section 19: Crito speaks of wishing notions to be true (p. 96). Lysicles
says that "our notions do, in this most learned and knowing age,
spread and multiply" (pp. 96–7).

Section 24: Crito refers to "your notions" (p. 106).

Alciphron, Dialogue 4

Section 13: Crito speaks of the "double face of the minute philosopher," saying it "is of no small use to propagate and maintain his
notions" (p. 158).

Alciphron, Dialogue 5

Section 19: Crito refers to the notions of the schoolmen (p. 194).

Section 27: Crito charges that if the notions of the deists are carefully
examined, they will "be found to include little of religion in them"
(p. 206).

Alciphron, Dialogue 6

Section 12: Lysicles refers to notions that are not agreeable to him. (p.
243)

Section 14: Lysicles says "My notions sit easy. I shall not engage in pedantic disputes about them" (p. 247).

Section 18: Lysicles says of Glaucus that "he is a peg too high for me in some of his notions" (p. 254).

Section 31: Crito rejects the notions of "a celebrated infidel" (p. 281).

Alciphron, Dialogue 7

Section 21: Crito: "Reason may oblige a man to believe against his inclinations; but why should a man quit salutary notions for others not less unreasonable than pernicious?" (p. 318)

Section 28: "How right the intentions of these men may be, replied Crito, I shall not say; but surely their notions are very wrong." (p. 325)

(2) Notions and common sense or those commonly accepted

New Theory of Vision

"The dedication": Berkeley says that "his thoughts have led him into some notions far out of common sense."

Dialogue One

p. 172: Hylas refers to men who advance notions that are repugnant to commonly received principles. Philonous has given up some of the sublime notions he learned at school, and he has replaced such metaphysical notions with the plain dictates of common sense.

p. 182: Philonous wants to discover whose notions are farthest from common sense.

Alciphron, Dialogue 5

Section 12: Crito refers to "the common notions of Englishmen" (p. 185).

(3) Notions linked with other terms

New Theory of Vision

Section 127: Refers to the "received notions and settled opinions of mankind."

Principles, Introduction

Section 15: Berkeley insists that "things, names and notions" are particular.

Principles

Section 5: The things we see and feel are "so many sensations, notions, ideas or impressions on the sense." None of these can be separated from perception.

Section 74: He asks what do we perceive "amongst all the ideas, sensations, notions" imprinted on the mind by sense or reflection. The answer is, not the materialist's substance.

Dialogue Three

p. 233: Philonous says that if he is to accept matter, he must have some reason for believing it to exist, but his sensations, ideas, notions, actions or passions do not give him any reason for saying material substance exists.

p. 243: Philonous: A notion that has no foundation in sense, reason or divine authority should be rejected.

Alciphron, Dialogue 1

Section 4: A reference to the free thinkers' account "of the numbers, progress and notions of their sect" (p. 38).

Section 5: A reference to "a wonderful variety of customs and rites, of institutions religious and civil, of notions and opinions very unlike and even contrary one to another" (pp. 39–40).

Section 9: Refers to "those whimsical notions of conscience, duty, principle, and the like, which fill a man's head with scruples, awe him with fears, and make him a more thorough slave than the horse he rides" (p. 44).

Alciphron, Dialogue 5

Section 10: Crito says there is no need to "inquire into all the rites and notions of the gentile world" (p. 183).

Section 12: Reference to "a survey of the prevailing notions and manners of this very country where we live, and compare them with those of our heathen predecessors" (p. 185).

Section 14: Crito speaks of Tully and the Romans, "the prevailing tenor of their lives and notions" (p. 188).

Section 18: Crito again refers to "a certain system of manners, customs, notions, rites, and laws, civil and religious" (p. 193).

Section 19: Reference to "many excellent rules and just notions, and useful truths in all those professions" (p. 194).

Section 22: Speaks of "notions, sentiments, and vices" (p. 200).

Section 27: Crito speaks of "those precepts, duties, and notions" accepted throughout the world (p. 205).

Section 28: "arguments and notions, which beget one another without end" (p. 207).

Section 30: Crito refers to "both things and notions placed to the account of liberty and property" (p. 209).

Section 32: Speaks of "a very different system of morals, politics, rights, and notions" (p. 213).

Alciphron, Dialogue 6

Section 2: Alciphron: "O Crito! That man may thank his stars to whom nature hath given a sublime soul, who can raise himself above popular opinions, and, looking down on the herd of mankind, behold them scattered over the surface of the whole earth, divided and subdivided into numberless nations and tribes, differing in notions and tenets, as in language, manners, and dress" (p. 220).

Section 7: Alciphron refers to "those French wits, who censure Homer because they do not find in him the style, notions, and manners of their own age and country" (p. 232).

Section 28: Crito refers to the "just notions, and useful truths in all those professions," i.e. law and physic (p. 275).

Alciphron, Dialogue 7

Section 7: Reference to "queries, disputes, perplexities, diversity of notions and opinions" about ideas of force (p. 296).

(4) Kinds of notions

(a) Absolute or relative

Principles, Section 114: Philosophers [scientists] who have a greater thought and "juster notions of the system of things," i.e., relative and absolute notion.

Dialogue Two, p. 223: Relative notion of things that are not directly perceived, for which we have no positive notion.

(b) Natural

Alciphron, Dialogue 1, section 14: Natural notions are those that are original in the mind and universal and invariable (p. 55).

Alciphron, Dialogue 3, section 3: Alciphron: "Men's first thoughts and natural notions are the best in moral matters" (p. 118).

Alciphron, Dialogue 7, section 19: A reference to the "received natural notions of guilt and merit, justice and reward"(p. 316).

(c) General or abstract

Principles, Introduction, section 10: Berkeley says he cannot form general notions by abstracting from particulars, nor do most men claim to have abstract notions. See also section 14 for abstract notions.

Principles, Introduction, section 17: Refers to "abstract natures and notions" in a reference to the debate about substance.

Principles, Introduction, section 19: The assumption that names stand for or refer to abstract notions.

Principles, section 74: The abstract indefinite notions of *being* and *occasion*.

Principles, section 100: Speaks of the supposed general ideas of goodness, justice, etc. He then refers to these as general notions.

Principles, section 143: He first talks of abstract ideas and then of abstract notions.

Dialogue Three, p. 247: The abstract notion of identity.

Alciphron, Dialogue 1, section 1: The "current general notion of the sect" (p. 32).

Alciphron, Dialogue 7, section 15: Speaks of "the perplexity of contradictions and abstracted notions, in all parts, whether of human science or divine faith" (p. 308).

Alciphron, Dialogue 7, section 18: Euphranor: "If I should suppose things spiritual to be corporeal, or refine things actual and real into general abstracted notions . . ." (p. 315).

Alciphron, Dialogue 7, section 20: A reference to "general notions and conclusions" (p. 316).

(5) Examples of specific notions

Principles, section 109: Speaks of enlarging our notions of grandeur, wisdom and beneficence of the Creator.

Principles, section 150: He refers to the heathens "who had not just notions of the omnipresence and infinite properties of God."

Dialogue One, p. 174, Philonous: Notions of God, virtue and truth.

Dialogue Three, p. 254, Philonous: Just notions of deity.

Alciphron, Dialogue 1, section 6: Religious notions; notion of a deity. (See also section 9.) (p. 41)

Alciphron, Dialogue 1, section 15: Alciphron refers to "the many different and inconsistent notions which men entertain of God and duty" (p. 58).

Alciphron, Dialogue 2, section 3: Notions of God and virtue (p. 69).

Alciphron, Dialogue 2, section 7: Religious notions. (See also sections 19, 20.) (p. 76)

Alciphron, Dialogue 2, section 20: A "notion of intriguing, and a notion of play." Also "a great notion of polite manners" (pp. 97, 98).

Alciphron, Dialogue 2, section 26: A false notion of liberty (p. 110).

Alciphron, Dialogue 3, section 13: The notion of "the beauty of pure, disinterested virtue" (p. 132).

Alciphron, Dialogue 3, section 14: Notions of good and evil (p. 136).

Alciphron, Dialogue 3, section 16: The received notions of God and providence (p. 140).

Alciphron, Dialogue 4, section 1: Notions govern mankind, e.g., a notion of God governing the world (p. 141).

Alciphron, Dialogue 5, section 3: Refers to the Greeks and the received notion of the gods (p. 177).

Alciphron, Dialogue 5, section 29: Lysicles speaks of the belief of God, virtue, and a future state. He calls these "such fine notions" (p. 208).

Alciphron, Dialogue 7, section 6: Euphranor, re force: "And to explain its nature, and distinguish the several notions or kinds of it, the terms *gravity, reaction, vis inertiae, vis insita, vis impressa, vis mortua, vis viva, impetus, momentum, solicitatio, conatus,* and divers other such like expressions have been used by learned men" (p. 294).

Alciphron, Dialogue 7, section 7: Notions of force and grace (p. 296).

Alciphron, Dialogue 7, section 10: Notions of faith, opinion and assent (p. 302).

Alciphron, Dialogue 7, section 16: Moral notion (p. 310).

Alciphron, Dialogue 7, section 18: Notions of certainty and necessity. Also, a notion of freedom (p. 315).

Alciphron, Dialogue 7, section 19: Notions of guilt and merit, praise and blame, accountable and unaccountable. Also, the "philosophic notions of liberty" and those of guilt and merit, justice and reward (p. 315).

Alciphron, Dialogue 7, section 20: The "only original true notions that we have of freedom, agent, or action" (p. 318).

The Guardian, Paper no. 88: The "most elevated Notions of Theology and Morality."

The Guardian, Paper no. 89: Speaks of notions of "the enjoyments of the Christian Paradise."

(6) Acquisition or source of notions

Alciphron, Dialogue 1

Section 5: Alciphron refers to the notions Euphranor "first sucked in with your milk, and which have been ever since nursed by parents, pastors, tutors, religious assemblies, books of devotion, and such methods of prepossessing men's minds" (p. 39).

Section 6: Education fills the tender mind of the child with religious notions, i.e., prejudices (p. 41).

Section 14: Alciphron speaks of "all those notions found in the human mind, which are the effect of custom and education" (p. 55).

Alciphron, Dialogue 4

Section 19: The "Received notions taken from holy Scripture and the light of nature" (p. 168).

Section 20: Thomas Aquinas is said to have observed that "our intellect gets its notions of all sorts of perfections from the creatures" (p. 168).

Alciphron, Dialogue 5

Section 35: Reference to notions "which pass for prejudices of a Christian education" (p. 217).

Alciphron, Dialogue 6

Section 1: People who "form their notions from conversation only, must needs have them very shattered and imperfect" (p. 219).

Section 8: Euphranor claims that "speech and style [are] instrumental to convey thoughts and notions, [which] . . . beget knowledge, opinion, and assent" (p. 233).

Section 24: Alciphron, re the Mosiac account: "if we are not attached singly to Moses, but take our notions from other writers, and the probability of things, we shall see good cause to believe, the Jews were only a crew of leprous Egyptians" (p. 266).

Section 26: A reference to "the notions and traditions in which" people are brought up (p. 271).

(7) Relation to Words and Language

New Theory of Vision

Section 73: Words suggest notions.

Section 120: Speaks of laying aside words in order to "consider the bare notions themselves."

Dialogue One

p. 174, Philonous says that words in a book mediately suggest to the mind "the notions of God, virtue, truth." Immediately, we only perceive the letters.

Dialogue Three

p. 246, Philonous charges philosophers with using words, rather than notions, to build their systems, words from common speech and language which can mislead.

Alciphron, Dialogue 2

Section 16: Lysicles says that "Pedants are governed by words and notions, while the wiser men of pleasure follow fact, nature, and sense" (p. 89).

Section 19: Euphranor recommends that we pay attention to notions rather than words, but he also places things over notions (p. 96).

Alciphron, Dialogue 4

Section 9: Euphranor speaking: "The littleness or faintness of appearance, or any other idea or sensation not necessarily connected with, or resembling distance, can no more suggest different degrees of distance, or any distance at all, to the mind which hath not experienced a connexion of the things signifying and signified, than words can suggest notions before a man hath learned the language." (p. 152)

Section 12: "Hence it is frequent for men to say, they see words, and notions, and things, in reading of a book; whereas in strictness they see only the characters, which suggest words, notions, and things" (p. 156).

Alciphron, Dialogue 5

Section 31: Lysicles says that "old customs and laws and national constitutions" are, as "we know and can demonstrate . . . only words and notions" (p. 212).

Section 32: "We all talk of just, and right, and wrong, and public good, and all those things. The names may be the same, but the notions and conclusions very different, perhaps diametrically opposite; and yet each may admit of clear proofs, and be inferred by the same way of reasoning" (p. 212).

Alciphron, Dialogue 7

Section 1: Alciphron says that an acute philosopher "hath no reverence for empty notions, or, to speak more properly, for mere forms of speech, which mean nothing, and are of no use to mankind" (p. 287).

(8) Confused, mistaken, absurd, misleading notions

New Theory of Vision

Section 80: If we do not distinguish between tangible and visual ideas, we are apt to create mistakes and confused notions.

Principles

Section 55: Speaks of a notion that is strongly adhered to, such as "the notion of the antipodes or the motion of the earth [which were once considered] . . . monstrous notions. Today, these notions have considerable support."

Section 96: When matter is expelled from nature, we get rid of all sorts of skeptical and impious notions.

Section 117: Re pure space: those who think space is God, or that there is a space that is eternal, infinite, etc. These are "pernicious and absurd notions."

Section 130: Speculations about infinity have produced some strange notions.

Dialogue One

p. 187, Philonous: Hylas's notion that colors are only unknown figures and motion of matter is a shocking notion.

Dialogue Two

p. 211, Philonous refers to those notions of Hylas which led into skepticism. Hylas's notion of reality denies the existence of sensible things.

Dialogue Three

p. 229, Philonous says Hylas's notions are wild and extravagant.

p. 233, Philonous: The very notion or definition of material substance contains a manifest repugnancy and inconsistency.

p. 243, Hylas: We should be wary of new notions because they can unsettle the mind.

Alciphron, Dialogue 1

Section 5: "Thus the shallow vulgar have their heads furnished with sundry conceits, principles, and doctrines, religious, moral, and political, all which they maintain with a zeal proportionable to their want of reason. On the other hand, those who duly employ their faculties in the search of truth, take especial care to weed out of their minds, and extirpate all such notions or prejudices as were planted in them before they arrived at the free and entire use of reason" (p. 39).

Section 9: Euphranor to Alciphron: "The gentlemen of your profession are, it seems, admirable weeders. You have rooted up a world of notions: I should be glad to see what fine things you have planted in their stead." (p. 45)

Section 11: Alciphron says those who read ancient authors in dead languages, often spend "a great part of their time . . . in learning words; which, when they have mastered with infinite pains, what do they get by it but old and obsolete notions, that are now quite exploded and out of use?" (p. 48)

Section 15: Reference to "crude notions" (p. 60).

Section 16: Slavish notions of religion and morality; and foolish notions (pp. 60, 61).

Alciphron, Dialogue 2

Section 3: Euphranor characterizes as "shocking" notions that are so contrary to "all laws, education, and religion" (p. 69).

Section 15: Old, stale and worn-out notions (p. 87).

Alciphron, Dialogue 4

Section 13: Euphranor: "Be pleased to recollect your own lectures upon prejudice, and apply them in the present case. Perhaps they may help you to follow where reason leads, and to suspect notions which are strongly riveted, without having been ever examined." (p. 158)

Alciphron, Dialogue 6

Section 13: Lysicles: "But what if I know the nature of the soul? What if I have been taught that whole secret by a modern free-thinker? a man of science who discovered it not by a tiresome introversion of his faculties, not by amusing himself in a labyrinth of notions, or stupidly thinking for whole days and nights together, but by looking into things and observing the analogy of nature" (p. 244).

Section 25: Slight and inconstant notions (p. 267).

Section 28: Alciphron speaks of "many false and fruitless notions engrafted" on Christianity by the wit of man (p. 275).

Section 32: Urges us to "check that disposition of his mind to conclude all those notions, groundless prejudices, with which it was imbued before it knew the reason of them." (p. 283)

Alciphron, Dialogue 7

Section 23: Euphranor speaks of extirpating wrong notions (p. 320).

Section 26: Crito speaks of Spinoza as "the great leader of our modern infidels, in whom are to be found many schemes and notions much admired and followed of late years; such as undermining religion, under the pretence of vindicating and explaining it" (p. 324).

Section 28: "As abstracted metaphysics, replied Crito, have always had a tendency to produce disputes among Christians, as well as other men, so it should seem that genuine truth and knowledge would allay this humour, which makes men sacrifice the undisputed duties of peace and charity to disputable notions. After all, said I, whatever may be said for reason, it is plain, the sceptics and infidels of the age are not to be cured by it" (pp. 325–6).

The Guardian
   Paper 39: Lifeless notions; "endless variety of Heathen notions";
      "Ancient Heathen notions."
   Paper 49: False notions "instilled by Custom and Education."
   Paper 88: The "gross Notions of the Heathen World."

(9) Notions of spirits, God and relations

Principles
   Section 89: "We comprehend our own existence by inward feeling or
      reflexion, and that of other spirits by reason. We may be said to have
      some knowledge or notion of our own minds, of spirits and active
      beings, whereof in the strict sense we have not ideas."
   Section 140: "In a large sense indeed, we may be said to have an idea,
      or rather a notion of *spirit*, that is, we understand the meaning of
      the word . . ."
   Section 142: The topic is our idea of spirit. Strictly, we cannot have an
      idea of an active being or of actions. We do, however, have a notion
      of them. That notion is what I know or understand by those words:
      "What I know, that I have some notion of." Berkeley also says that
      "idea" and "notion" may be interchangeable, but it is better to keep
      them separate. Also, we have notions of the relations and habitude
      of things: "all relations including an act of the mind, we cannot so
      properly be said to have an idea, but rather a notion."
Dialogue Three
   p. 233, Philonous: This is the main passage where he says "I have a
      notion of spirit, though I have not, strictly speaking, an idea of it."
      In this same passage, he remarks that "the being of my self, that is,
      my own soul, mind or thinking principle, I evidently know by
      reflexion."

III

It has been the use of the term "notion" in this last group that has
received almost all the commentators' attention. Flage's detailed study[9]
mentions in passing notions of perception and causation (p. 154) and

---

[9] Daniel E. Flage, *Berkeley's Doctrine of Notions: A Reconstruction Based on His Theory of Meaning*
(London: Croom Helm, 1987). See also his article, "Relative Ideas and Notions," in *Minds, Ideas,
and Objects: Essays on the Theory of Representation in Modern Philosophy*, ed. Phillip D. Cummins and
Günter Zöller (Abascadero, Calif.: Ridgeview, 1992), pp. 235–53.

notions of the operations of the mind (p. 155), but it is my group 9 which is the subject of his analysis. Bracken wrote in 1974 that "Notions are used by Berkeley when he talks about things which cannot be expressed in the language of ideas."[10] Bracken does not say that is the *only* occasion when Berkeley uses the term. My inventory shows that the group 9 use is just a very small percentage of the use of "notion" and "notions" in Berkeley's writings. A. C. Lloyd recognizes that there is a wide use of these terms and a technical use, but he offers no examples of the wide use.[11] Flage speaks of "the shroud of mystery surrounding" Berkeley's doctrine of the special, technical use, a mystery which he claims to dissolve. Notions are, he says, intentional acts, although he recognizes that that use is clearly linked with meaning. Lloyd argues that notions are acts, not intuitions, the only alternatives he offers. Winkler offers a more general suggestion: to have a notion is to be able to think of something or to understand something.[12] This general description places the stress on the acts of thinking and understanding, rather than on what is thought about or understood: but, of course, Winkler recognizes that Berkeley says we think with notions, e.g., when we think of God, spirits, or relations.

Winkler's description points the way towards a more general use of notions, a use that my groups 1–8 illustrate. Berkeley remarks, in the dedication to his *New Theory of Vision*, that he holds some notions contrary to common sense (group 2). I would think we could cite as such notions in that work his claim that we see immediately only light and colors, that we do not see the same object that we touch. From group 1, his notions would include the *esse est percipi* principle, his turning ideas into things, and his important distinction between "existing in the mind" and "being a property of the mind."[13] The dualism and corpuscularianism of Hylas's position is another notion. Under my group 4, there are absolute and relative notions, natural notions, general and abstract notions. Among specific notions listed in my group 5 are: grandeur, wisdom, virtue, truth, duty, intrigue, play, liberty, beauty, good and evil and many more. Group 8 identifies notions that are considered bad from someone's point of view, or notions that were once accepted but are now known to be false. In the *Principles*, those who said space was God, or who

---

[10] Harry M. Bracken, *Berkeley* (London: Macmillan, 1974), p. 135.
[11] "The Self in Berkeley's Philosophy," *Essays on Berkeley: A Tercentennial Celebration*, ed. John Foster and Howard Robinson (Oxford: Clarendon Press, 1985), p. 264.
[12] Kenneth P. Winkler, *Berkeley: An Interpretation* (Oxford: Clarendon Press, 1989), p. 279.
[13] This distinction is succinctly expressed in his *Philosophical Commentaries*, no. 878. It also occurs in the *Principles* and the *Dialogues*.

made space eternal, are said to have pernicious and absurd notions. Other entries in that group give us a range of such mistaken, shocking, misleading notions. Notions of the sect of Free Thinkers were particularly objectionable to Berkeley. This group of notions is one of the largest on my inventory. Some of these notions can be traced to education and early influences, fostered by custom and tradition (group 6). Group 7 also indicates that notions are suggested by words, words that can sometimes mislead us. Berkeley urges us to put words aside sometimes so that we can examine the notions themselves (bare notions, he calls them in one passage): the veil of words. *Alciphron* contains many remarks on the relations between words and notions. The various series of other words in which the term "notion" occurs (group 3) are of special interest. Notions are associated with opinions, they appear along with sensations, impressions and ideas. A system of morals, politics, rights and notions is another series where notions appear.

Does this wider and rather extensive use of the term permit us to draw any conclusions or form any opinions on (a) the more specialized use in group 9, (b) the special use of "idea" instead of "thing" for sensible object, or (c) the relation between notions and ideas? With this inventory of uses of "notion" and "notions" before us from groups 1–8, I do not see how we could say those notions were acts, intentional or otherwise. The notions Berkeley held about vision, the notions of virtue, good and evil, etc.: all these are contents of mental acts (acts of thinking, believing, doubting), the thoughts, opinions, ideas (in the nonspecial sense) that Berkeley, Hylas and Alciphron had about those qualities and principles. Group 9 notions do not strike me as being any different. The notions of God or those of mind or self contain what I know, think, or believe about God, minds or spirits. Berkeley's notion of God contains the property of omniscience, for example. His notion of spirit contains the property of being active. When Berkeley thinks about God, he forms notions about him. Thinking is an act, the notion is the content of that act.

IV

Locke indicated that the terms "idea, notions, phantasms" were different ways of referring to whatever is the object of the mind when it thinks. Berkeley employs the term "notion" in that sense, as the uses in all my groups confirm. He also occasionally uses the term "idea" in the same sense, for example in group 3 (*Principles*, section 142; *Dialogue Three*, p.

233), or when he says that "idea" and "notion" could be interchanged (*Principles*, section 140). But Locke's term "idea" is given a new and restricted sense in Berkeley's account of the external world and our knowledge of it. He could just have used the term "thing," as he says in several places, but that term usually covers more than sensible things. He wanted a special term, one that still designated objects of thought or properties, but a term freed of the usual mental features. He did not want the term "idea" to refer to a mode of mind, to a subjective property, while at the same time he wanted it not to be entirely independent of perceptual awareness. "Idea" in this special sense can be characterized as Berkeley characterized extension in his *Philosophical Commentaries*: "Extension tho it exist only in the Mind, yet is no Property of the Mind" (No. 878). He explicitly employed this distinction for his term "idea" in the third of the *Three Dialogues*: ideas *exist in* the mind, "not by way of mode or property, but as a thing perceived in that which perceives it" (p. 237). Section 49 of the *Principles* makes the same point, draws the same distinction. He replies to the objection that "if extension and figure exist only in the mind, it follows that the mind is extended and figured; since extension is a mode or attribute, which (to speak with the Schools) is predicated of the subject in which it exists." His answer is that "these qualities are in the mind only as they are perceived by it, that is, not by way of *mode* or *attribute*, but only by way of *idea*." Those qualities are not predicated of the mind, but they exist in, are perceived by the mind. Whether particular qualities or a group of qualities (a sensible object), they exist in, are perceived by, but are not properties of the mind.

There are many passages where Berkeley addresses this notion of existence in the mind. As early as section 2 of the *Principles*, he gives an unequivocal explication: by mind, spirit or self he means a thing (a being) distinct from ideas but that "wherein they [ideas] exist, or, which is the same thing, whereby they are perceived." Section 6 links "actually perceived by me" with "exist in my mind." Section 7 tells us that it is all one (i.e., the same) to have an idea and to perceive; that is why the ideas of extension, figure and motion, as well as colors and tastes, cannot exist in an unperceiving substance (sections 9, 15). Section 23 gives us another specific link (equation?) between "are apprehended by" and "exist in" the mind. Section 33 identifies sensations as ideas and then states "they exist in the mind, or are perceived by it." Section 34 is especially important and outspoken. In that section, he addresses the objection that on his account (on his notion) "all that is real and substantial in Nature is banished out of the world: and instead thereof a chimerical scheme of ideas takes place." The importance of this section lies in its clear contrast between his meaning of "existence in the mind" and what he designates as a "purely notional" account assumed by the objection. A notional existence in the mind would be one where the ideas *are* predicated of the mind, they would be properties of the mind. The being of objects in the mind is not a notional existence. It is, as it was for Descartes, an epistemic existence. *Esse est percipi*, "to be is to be perceived," is clearly a translation of "to be is to exist in the mind."

Several passages in the *Third Dialogue* reiterate the equivalence between "exist in the mind" and "is known, apprehended, perceived" by the mind. For example, "Farther, I know what I mean, when I affirm that there is a spiritual substance or support of ideas, that is, that a spirit knows and perceives ideas" (p. 234). Or again p. 235: "But then to a Christian it cannot surely be shocking to say, the real tree existing without his mind is truly known and comprehended by (that is, exists in) the infinite mind of God." A later passage (p. 250) is quite explicit. Philonous explains to Hylas that "when I speak of objects as existing in the mind or imprinted on the senses; I would not be understood in the gross literal sense, as when bodies are said to exist in a place, or a seal to make an impression upon wax. My meaning is only that the mind comprehends or perceives them."

When Philonous explains to Hylas that it is a contradiction to say "an idea exists in an unthinking [& unperceiving] thing," the contradiction becomes clear when we substitute "is perceived by" for "exists in": "an idea [i.e., a sensible object] is perceived by an unthinking [& unperceiving] thing." When Philonous says that an idea can only be like another idea, that substitution yields: "a sensible thing can only be like another sensible thing." A sensible object differs from a perceiving being. Thus, if we fail to notice Berkeley's special sense of "idea," to say "I have an idea of self or mind" would be to say a sensible object can be a means for knowing or understanding self or mind. Ideas in his special sense are not modes of mind, as they would have to be (and as they were for Locke and Descartes) were they the means for knowing spirit. There is no special mental property giving us a knowledge of sensible objects; we know, or at least become aware of them, immediately when we look or feel.[14] For other objects of knowledge, thought, imagination we do apparently need something more besides an act of thinking, imagining,

---

[14] For the details supporting this claim of nonmediated access to ordinary objects, see my *Perception and Reality*, pp. 146–52.

etc. Notions are the contents of thought, the means by which we come to understand the words which suggest the notions. Philonous says that words in a book mediately suggest to the mind "the notions of God, virtue, truth" (p. 174). We see the letters of the words immediately (see group 7).

v

We can now say, in answer to the relation between notions and ideas ((c) p. 94 above), that there are no relations between ideas in Berkeley's special sense and notions, no relation, that is, between sensible things (which are what ideas are for Berkeley) and notions. The distinction between "exist in" and "being a property of" speaks to (b): "idea" for Berkeley's purposes is better than "thing." As for (a), the supposed specialized use of the term "notion," the long list of occurrences of "notion" and "notions" in my inventory shows that the group 9 use of those terms is no different from the uses in groups 1–8. Berkeley retained the term "notion" in Locke's general sense along with "idea," as designating whatever is the object of the mind when it thinks. When he remarks in *Principles,* section 142, that he could have used "idea" when referring to spirit or God but he thinks it better to keep those terms separate, he is using the term "idea" in both its general and the special sense. The separation of "idea" from "notion" is necessitated because he has given the term "idea" a new sense (to use an expression from Hume) as the very things themselves. Locke's ideas have been turned into things, as Philonous explains to Hylas. The new use of that term is the reason why it would be improper to say we have an idea of mind or spirit or God. It would be equally improper to use the term "idea" instead of "notion" in the examples from my groups 1–8, except for those few places I have noted where he does use "idea" in the general, Lockean sense.

Focusing attention on the supposed special use of the term "notion" for God, minds, and relations diverts attention from the extensive use of that term for many other contents and objects of thought. It also obscures the fact that Berkeley uses that term as Locke did the term "idea." More importantly, focusing attention on my group 9 use of "notion" and overlooking the general use of that term in Berkeley's writings makes it difficult to appreciate the very special, perhaps radical, sense Berkeley gives to the term "idea." In saying he has not turned things into ideas, Berkeley is saying he has not given things a *notional existence* in, and made them a property of, the mind. Rather, he has turned ideas into things and, if we want to retain the notion of existence, we must say he has given them an *epistemic existence* in the mind. But that phrase means that Berkeley is defining the term "object" as that which is perceived and known. Ideas in his special sense are the things, the ordinary things of everyday life, that are discovered in our perceptual experiences through our sensings and perceivings. They are what appears to us, the sensory appearances of the known world. Ontologically, Berkeley's objects are located between subjective states and the insensible corpuscular matter of scientists and of most philosophers.

6

Hume's "appearances" and his vocabulary of awareness

Our ideas are, somehow, the objects themselves, and so they are no mere representations of reality.
Robert Pasnau, *Theories of Cognition in the Later Middle Ages* (1997), p. 299.

A variety of items in Hume's *Treatise* are said to appear to the soul or mind. Sensations, passions and emotions appear in the soul (p. 1), pain and pleasure make their appearance in the mind (p. 118), impressions and ideas "make their way into our thoughts or consciousness" (p. 1). An alternative phrase for "appear to or in the soul or mind" is "to be present with or to the mind." When an impression "has been present with the mind," we find that its next appearance is as an idea (p. 8). Impressions cannot "become present to the mind" without a specific degree of quantity or quality (p. 10). Operations of the mind are "most intimately present to us" (*Enquiry*, p. 13). Hume does not say that when a sensation, emotion, pain or pleasure appears to the soul, we are aware of that sensation, emotion, pain and pleasure. Nor does he make explicit that when impressions or ideas are present with the mind (sometimes it is "perceptions" that are present with the mind), we are conscious of them. But I believe "being conscious or aware" of what is present with the mind and what appears to the soul or mind is implicit in what he says.

Still other items are said to appear to the mind. For example, a line "has in its appearance in the mind, a precise degree of quantity and quality" (p. 19). Right lines have a particular appearance to the mind (p. 50). Right lines and a plain surface are said to have a general appearance (pp. 50–1). Colored points have a particular manner of appearance (p. 34). Time is said not to make its appearance to the mind alone, by itself (p. 35), it is always "conjoined with a succession of changeable objects" (p. 36). Sounds also make their appearance in a certain manner (p. 36), and qualities are present to us and have an appearance (p. 91). Tastes, smells, colors are said to be "co-temporary in their appearance in the mind," such that, upon the appearance of one of these qualities in the mind, our thought is "turned to" the others (p. 237). In general, causes and effects, some of the more pervasive items of appearance, also make their appearance to the mind, enabling us to move in thought from one to the other (pp. 104, 128).

The most important items that are present with the mind or make their appearance to the mind are impressions and ideas, perceptions generally, and objects. If we take a more detailed look at some of these occurrences, we may be able to fill out Hume's account of perceptual awareness.

I

The early pages of the *Treatise* sketch some of the relations between ideas and impressions. Simple ideas in their *first* appearance are derived from simple impressions (p. 4); that is the order of their first appearance: impressions before ideas (p. 5). Illustrating this sequence, he speaks of presenting an object to a child in order to give the child an idea of scarlet or sweet or bitter, explaining that "presenting an object" will "convey to" the child the impressions of scarlet, sweet, bitter. The result would be the first appearance of those impressions to the child, the child would then perceive those qualities. From "appear," Hume moves to "perceive." Once an impression "has been present with the mind, it again makes its appearance there as an idea" (p. 8). The impression becomes an idea. Impressions also prepare the way for ideas of memory and imagination; those ideas will not make their appearance to the mind without that preparation (p. 9). Not only do impressions *become* ideas, ideas of the imagination *make their appearance* in impressions (p. 33). More generally, "all the perceptions of the mind are double, and appear both as impressions and ideas" (pp. 2–3).

In a later passage, Hume speaks of the appearance of an object in an impression. He is there writing about the way appearances of an object which have been frequently conjoined with the appearance of another object result in our making an easy transition from the idea of one to the idea of the other object (pp. 115–18). Those ideas make their appearance in the mind (p. 116). How are we to understand the notion of an object *appearing in* an impression? Is it that objects *appear to* the senses, that the sensory appearance is the object as it is present to the senses? The appearance of the object takes a sensory form, the appearance in its sensory form then *becomes* an idea. Later still in the *Treatise*, Hume speaks of objects "discovering themselves" to the senses (p. 167). That passage is from the section on the idea of necessary connection, his claim being that necessary connection is a quality or feature of perceptions, not of objects. When objects discover themselves to the senses, specific internal impressions make their appearance at the same time. Because of this conjunction of objects discovering themselves and internal impressions appearing to the mind, "the mind has a propensity to spread itself on external objects" (p. 167), that is, to ascribe the impressions or qualities to the object.[1] Since these impressions (e.g., of sounds, tastes) do not have a location in space, they "exist no where," these impressions or qualities have an existence, but not a spatial one, they cannot belong to spatially located objects.

The internality of some impressions is also found in the section on modern philosophy. There, he cites the impressions of color, sound, heat, cold, saying that they "arise from causes which no way resemble them" (p. 227). Modern philosophers go on to claim a different status for other qualities; the primary qualities, changes in objects are due to those qualities. Hume believes that the distinction between primary and secondary qualities fails to explain the operation of external objects, but more importantly, that distinction leads to an extravagant skepticism. "If colours, sounds, tastes, and smells be merely perceptions, nothing we can conceive is possest of a real, continu'd, and independent existence; not even motion, extension and solidity, which are the primary qualities chiefly insisted on" (p. 228).

II

I think we can say that in this last remark, Hume is speaking in his own voice, that is the view that emerges from his analysis in the section on skepticism with regard to the senses. It is also the view he endorses in the Conclusion to Book I, although he regrets that he has been unable to find any reasoning to support it. The qualities that present themselves to our senses, the sensations or perceptions we have of those qualities, are not merely subjective or internal events: they have some relation to continued independent existences. Similarly, I think we can say in Hume's voice that objects are not *merely* perceptions, but the relation between them is intimate and unavoidable. The term "perception" designates the

---

[1] See Hume's *Enquiry concerning the Principles of Morals*, where he distinguishes between reason, which "discovers objects as they really stand in nature," and taste which is a productive faculty "gilding or staining all natural objects with the colours, borrowed from internal sentiment" (p. 294).

class to which impressions and ideas belong. Even in a single sentence, Hume will sometimes alternate between impressions and perceptions. Just one example: "When we have been accustom'd to observe a constancy in certain impressions, and have found, that the perception of the sun or ocean, for instance, returns upon us after an absence or annihilation, with like parts and in a like order, as at its first appearance, we are not apt to regard the interrupted perceptions as different" (p. 199). Strictly, those interrupted perceptions, the broken impressions, are not identical, but we tend to overlook that fact. The phrase, "the perception of the sun or ocean," may refer to our awareness of the sun or ocean by means of the impressions we have from our senses, but the term "perceptions" in that sentence refers to the interrupted impressions, the interrupted appearances. This passage continues by talking of "impressions", switching still later to "interrupted perceptions," and "broken appearances" (p. 200).

There are a number of other passages on pp. 200–2 which speak of interrupted or resembling perceptions, but at this point in the *Treatise* we have entered that part of Hume's analysis of the ordinary view which, on his account, uses the terms "perception" and "object" interchangeably. For the ordinary person, objects *are* perceptions, and perceptions *are* objects. Hume even has the generality of mankind equating "the very sensations which enter [the mind?] by the eye or ear," with the "true object" (p. 207). On this view, to say perceptions appear, or to talk of the appearances of perceptions, is the same as to say objects appear to us. So from page 202 to page 211, any reference to appearances of perceptions is to be understood as being the same as the appearances of objects, the appearances of hats, shoes, stones.

III

There are many passages in earlier sections which have objects appearing to us and references to the appearances of objects. Specific objects are mentioned frequently in Hume's discussion of equality and inequality. Some of these objects are just objects of our thought, such as lines and surfaces. Right lines and curves are said to be objects of the mind (p. 49), meaning the subject of our attention, or even of our senses as we look at a drawn line or figure. Other objects are bodies, physical bodies as objects of perception and knowledge. The phrase "external objects" occurs throughout his discussion. Sometimes in his discussion of equality, Hume makes use of physical objects (pp. 47–52). The mind is said to be able "at one view to determine the properties of bodies" (p. 47). In his discussion of space, he refers to our perception "when two luminous bodies appear to the eye" (p. 57). The difference between darkness and the appearance of two or more objects is said to consist in "the objects themselves, and in the manner they affect our senses" (p. 58). He also refers there to tangible objects and to our perceiving such objects. Visible objects also affect our senses. Sensible objects affect our fancy (p. 100). I take the term "affect" to be a causal word.

Part III, section I of the *Treatise*, on Knowledge, refers to objects appearing in a place, and of "the qualities of objects as they appear to us" (pp. 69–70). The reference on p. 71 to "the general appearance of objects" may include lines and curves, but it also seems to apply to spatial objects, to bodies. Section VI refers to "any species of objects" which are "found by experience to be constantly united with an individual of another species" (p. 93). His discussion of the probability of causes speaks of "the view of an object," a "conjunction of objects," and of the effects that attend an object (pp. 132–3). When writing on the idea of necessary connection, Hume begins by turning *his* eye "to two objects supposed to be plac'd" in a causal relation (p. 155), and he refers to the appearance of one of the objects (p. 156). I noted above the passage which has objects discovering themselves to the senses (p. 167). The section on skepticism with regard to the senses, prior to Hume adopting the ordinary way of speaking, refers to the "past and present appearances" of objects (p. 197), of "two kinds of objects in their past appearances to the senses" (pp. 197–8), and objects are said to have "a certain coherence even as they appear to our senses" (p. 199).

The *Enquiry concerning Human Understanding* also has frequent references to objects applied to a sense organ and exciting a particular sensation (p. 20), objects presented to a man (pp. 27–8); Hume speaks of immediately observing "a continual succession of objects" (p. 42). He also repeats the phrase we found in the *Treatise*, objects that are immediately present to memory and the senses (p. 74). The "actual presence of an object" is mentioned on p. 52, and the presence of an object is said to excite the idea of another object (p. 55). Objects that have "in our eyes been frequently conjoined" are referred to later (p. 159). External objects appear to the senses (p. 64); observation and experience is the way we learn about objects (p. 68). He also speaks of looking about us toward external objects (p. 63). He refers to "events which appear in the course of nature, and the operation of external objects" (p. 86; see also p. 93). There is a locution Hume employs which seems to be another way of referring to external objects, "natural objects." In the *Treatise*, there is one such occurrence in a note on p. 461. Several others are found in the *Enquiry concerning Human Understanding*. For example, the presenting of natural objects is mentioned on p. 17, the discovery of similarities among natural objects is cited on p. 36, we are said to learn "the qualities of natural objects by observing the effects which result from them" (p. 39). Later in the *Enquiry* he considers the situation "when any natural object or event is presented" (p. 74). There is also a reference in the *Treatise* to "material objects" (p. 410). The collection of particles of matter is also mentioned in several passages (e.g. p. 401), and the notion of matter receives some discussion in various places.

Spread throughout both books are references to various objects, external objects that presumably discover themselves to us, that we look at and observe, that are present to our senses: clocks and watches, a dye, billiard balls, peaches and pears, writing paper, a table, houses, fields, a burning fire, pieces of marble, bread that nourishes, a candle, a glass of wine, rhubarb and opium, a frog, fish, stones (to mention just a few). When we look outward to any of these objects, when we present some of them to a child so that the child may experience a specific sensation, can we say what Hume's account is of looking and showing bodies and external objects? That physical objects such as those listed here are integral to Hume's account would seem beyond dispute. That we all do believe in the existence of such objects, that there is both an external and internal world is a conviction we all have, even after the tensions and contortions we experience when we try to escape the skepticism resulting from the debates of philosophers about our knowledge of the external world (*Treatise*, p. 218). Such was the conclusion to the section on skepticism with regards the senses, as it was the assertion at the beginning of that section: it is "vain to ask, *Whether there be body or not*? That is a point we must take for granted in all our reasonings" (*Treatise*, p. 187). The question is, what is the body that we must take for granted, what is its nature? There may be two further questions: (a) what can we understand bodies to be, perhaps even, what are we entitled to say about them, and (b) does the answer to any of these questions lie with science or common sense, with philosophical theory or with our ordinary beliefs?

IV

Within this section of the *Treatise* (Book I, Part IV, section III), Hume makes several forthright statements about seeing physical objects, state-

ments that seem to be ones he accepts. But since this section addresses
the debates among philosophers about our knowledge of the external
world, we may have to be cautious in ascribing these remarks to Hume.
Still, he says firmly that "properly speaking, 'tis not our body we perceive, when we regard our limbs and members, but certain impressions,
which enter by the senses" (p. 191). The term "regard" is somewhat
curious. The Appendix to the *Treatise* uses the word "view": "When I
view this table and that chimney, nothing is present to me but particular
perceptions, which are of a like nature with all the other perceptions" (p.
634). In that passage, Hume identifies this distinction between what I
view and what is present with me as the doctrine of philosophers. What
is it to regard or view a leg or arm? Is it the same as using my eyes to look
at my arm, perhaps to discover whether I have cut myself on a rose bush
or with my pruning shears? Legs and arms are, at this stage in Hume's
account, still distinct from the impressions we have, even though we are
not able to perceive (see?) the legs or arms. We can "regard" them but
not "perceive" them.[2] Put differently, what appears to the mind are perceptions, not arms and legs (p. 193). At least, so philosophy claims: "For
philosophy informs us, that every thing which appears to the mind, is
nothing but a perception, and is interrupted and dependent on the
mind" (p. 193). Later in the section, he gives what seems to be a clear
explication of seeing and feeling: "External objects are seen, and felt,
and become present to the mind; that is, they acquire such a relation to
a connected heap of perceptions, as to influence them very considerably
in augmenting their number by present reflexions and passions" (p. 207).
For objects to be present to the mind means that they add more perceptions to the mind. So the phrase, "present to the mind," has two different
senses: one for objects, the other for perceptions. Objects influence
(cause?) the mind to add more perceptions to those already existing. The
action of objects thus results in "storing the memory with ideas." In this
remark, objects seem not themselves to be perceptions, they are percep-
tion-causing. In this paragraph Hume was offering an explanation of
how, on the view of objects and perceptions being the same, a perception that appears and disappears could be an object, in the sense of a
continued and uninterrupted being. Embedded in this passage is the
question of the cause of our perceptions, what it is that brings it about
that an object or perception is present to the mind. That question

---

[2] Perhaps in Hume's distinction between perceiving and regarding, we are hearing an echo of
Malebranche's distinction between "voir" and "regarder." For a discussion of this distinction in
Malebranche, see my *Perceptual Acquaintance*, pp. 44–7.

receives no answer. The previous page has all mankind and philosophers (most of the time) taking "their perceptions to be their only objects," and he goes on to say mankind and philosophers "suppose, that the very being, which is intimately present to the mind, is the real body or material existence" (p. 206). The language here is very close to Descartes's talk of the objective reality of ideas, the *being* of objects existing in the mind. Hume is saying that the very being of bodies is present to us by means of our perceptions, the being of the object is contained in our perceptions. As he goes on to develop the ordinary view, this similarity with Descartes becomes clear.

That striking remark on p. 206 about the *being* of objects is Hume's way of articulating the ordinary belief in a single, not a double existence. Perceptions are objects. At least the perceptions that are present to the mind are the very things themselves as known or perceived. The explication of seeing and feeling on p. 207, which drew a distinction between our perceptions and objects that influence our stock of perceptions, seems not to appear on p. 206. The two different versions of "present to the mind" implied in the p. 207 passage also seem to disappear from the general claim made on p. 197, prior to the passage accepting the single existence view of ordinary people: "nothing is ever really present to the mind, besides its own perceptions." Or is it that the distinction between "really present" (or perhaps "intimately present") and another way of being present to the mind is still in the background? We can apply some of Hume's language to Descartes's account: ideas (perceptions) are present to the mind as modes of the mind, but those same ideas present objects to the mind, they make the object also present to the mind (now to use Berkeley's language), not as modes or properties of the mind, but as perceptions. Hume's claim about what is "really present" to the mind was also made much earlier, in the section on the idea of "existence and external existence," where the echoes of Descartes's objective reality are heard again: "We may observe, that 'tis universally allow'd by philosophers, and is besides pretty obvious of itself, that nothing is ever really present with the mind but its perceptions or impressions and ideas" (p. 67).[3] In that passage, he adds most importantly that "external objects become known to us only by those perceptions they occasion." What is present with the mind are perceptions, but objects are known (are epistemically contained in the perceptions, to use Cartesian language) by the

---

[3] Cf. *Treatise*, Book III, Part I, section I: "It has been observ'd, that nothing is present to the mind but its perceptions; and that all the actions of seeing, hearing, judging, loving, hating, and thinking, fall under this denomination" (p. 456).

perceptions. Again, the term "really" may preserve another sense of "present to" when objects discover themselves to our senses, when, we might say, they present themselves to our eyes or hands, thereby "causing" the mind to have perceptions. More strongly and more Cartesian, objects present themselves to the mind in the perceptions they occasion.[4]

v

Whether my suggested parallel between Hume's and Descartes's talk of the being of objects in the mind is accepted, I think we can say with confidence that Hume's world contains at least external (natural) objects and internal perceptions. His account of perceptual awareness assumes the workings of neurophysiology, just as it assumes the existence of external objects. In the section on skepticism and the senses, he says that perceptions are "dependent on our organs and the disposition of our nerves and animal spirits" (p. 211). When the mind fails to operate normally, part of the cause is that the animal spirits "are diverted from their natural course" (p. 188). He offers a very detailed account of the workings of the animal spirit physiology, both when the mind is successful and when it fails, in the dissection of the brain passage (pp. 60–1).[5] Other passages in the *Treatise* indicate Hume's use and acceptance of the animal spirit physiology.[6] That physiology was generally accepted by most writers on perception in the eighteenth century, but it was largely theoretical (as were the other versions of the physiology of the body).[7] So the

---

[4] The term used by Hume, "occasion," may also be an echo of Descartes, a possible distinction between occasion and cause. Hume does not address the nature of the occasioning or causing. As I mentioned in chapter 2, Descartes suggested that the relation between the physical and mental was a function of brain motions acting as signs to the mind.

[5] See also the *Enquiry*, p. 66: "We learn from anatomy, that the immediate object of power in voluntary action, is not the member itself which is moved, but certain muscles and nerves, and animal spirits, and, perhaps, something still more minute and more unknown, through which the motion is successively propagated, ere it reach the member itself whose motion is the immediate object of volition." See also *Treatise*, Book II, Part III, section v, pp. 422–3: "Whether the soul applies itself to the performance of any action, or the concept of any object, to which it is not accustom'd, there is a certain unpliableness in the faculties, and a difficulty of the spirit's moving in their new direction." This difficulty, he says, "excites the spirits."

[6] For example: pp. 28, 98, 123, 135, 185, 203, 210, 230, 269, 275, 290, 353, 419, 424. There are a number of references to this physiology in his *Dissertation on the Passions*, where "animal spirits" is usually shortened to "spirits." See *Works*, 4 vols., ed. T. H. Green and T. H. Grose (London, 1874–5), vol. 4, pp. 163–5.

[7] For some discussion of this physiology in the seventeenth and eighteenth centuries, see my *Perceptual Acquaintance* and *Thinking Matter*. See also John Sutton's detailed discussion in his *Philosophy and Memory Traces: Descartes to Connectionism* (Cambridge: Cambridge University Press, 1998), esp. pp. 21–106.

existence of the perceiver's body is quite explicit in Hume's *Treatise*, that body is one example of external objects.

He does not say why it is that "we must take for granted in all our reasonings" that "there be body," but it is clear from the many examples of, references to, and use made of physical objects in the *Treatise* and in the *Enquiry* that he has taken for granted the existence of such objects. Those objects are necessary if we are to experience sensations, feel pain, see colors, shapes, or regard our body. He comes close to saying physical objects *cause* us to have perceptions and to experience appearances, although there is no account offered of the process from objects to nerves and brain, still less is there an account of the relation between the physiology of nerves and brain and our awareness of perceptions. Words such as "influence" and "affect" do not specify the nature of the influencing or affecting. Although the claim that objects cause us to have perceptions has come in for some debate of late, he is more explicit about saying those objects have specific powers, for example, bread has the power to nourish, opium has the power to make us sleep, medicine has curative powers. The great number of references in both books to secret springs and principles, to powers, would seem to indicate unequivocally that Hume's world, the world in which we as perceivers exist, is filled with physical objects, events and processes. Our body itself has "many secret powers" that "lurk" in it (*Enquiry*, p. 87). The difficulty is that this rich world of power objects, of objects which operate by principles, only some of which natural philosophy has discovered (Hume mentions elasticity, gravity, cohesion of parts, and communication of motion by impulse[8]), is not accessible by experience and observation. Our knowledge is limited to the appearances, to the perceptions that appear to the mind. Just as "any hypothesis that pretends to discover the ultimate original principles of human nature, ought at first to be rejected as presumptuous and chimerical," so I would assume, any claim of a discovery of the ultimate original principles of physical nature ought at first to be rejected for the same reasons (*Treatise*, p. xvii). Whether the phrase "at first" suggests a later possible acceptance is unclear. It just may mean reject the claim right away, out of hand. What would be rejected is not the notion of ultimate original principles, but the claim that they have been discovered. Human knowledge is limited to appearances. Early on, Hume explains that his intention in the *Treatise* "never was to penetrate

---

[8] These, Hume says, "are probably the ultimate causes and principles which we shall ever discover in nature," *Enquiry concerning Human Understanding*, p. 30.

into the nature of bodies, or explain the secret causes of their operations" (p. 64). Such an "enterprise is beyond the reach of human understanding"; we can never "pretend to know body otherwise than by those
external properties, which discover themselves to the senses" (p. 64).

The search for general principles is quite proper; Hume thought he
had discovered some that explain the workings of the mind and human
nature. He only insisted that, as he reaffirmed in the *Abstract*, "we can
never arrive at the ultimate principles" but it is "a satisfaction to go as
far as our faculties will allow us" (p. 646). With reference to bodies,
Hume affirms in the *Abstract* that "The powers by which bodies operate,
are entirely unknown" (p. 652; cf. *Treatise*, p. 102), including, I would say,
how bodies operate on the perceiver's nerves and brain. Thus, the causation of perception, of appearances, is not part of Hume's account, even
though it seems clear that perceptions do not become present to the
mind by anything that perceivers do, certainly not solely by anything
done by perceivers. Our faculties do have powers. Hume offers some
principles which he thinks explain their workings, but the action of our
faculties takes place after some impressions or ideas have become
present with the mind, after we are perceptually aware of some appearance. The imagination is for Hume a "magical" faculty, but not even it
can, I think, initiate perceptions prior to some sense awareness.

VI

The components of perceptual awareness for Hume, the various items
required for such awareness, include on the side of the perceiver: a mind
or soul; faculties such as reason, imagination and memory; thoughts;
consciousness; perceptions, ideas and impressions; sensations; passions;
and actions such as looking, regarding and viewing. Perceptual awareness also requires external objects in space, some process from those
objects to specific sense organs, a consequent neurophysiological action
in nerves and brain, a receptive mind (or perceiver), and some undefined
process from brain events to awareness.[9] This last component in the perceptual process was the one that gave trouble to most of the seventeenth-
and eighteenth-century philosophers. Hume just seems to ignore it; he
ignores it for the same reason that physiological explanations are only

---

[9] Cf. *Treatise*, p. 230: "An object, that presses upon any of our members, meets with resistance; and
that resistance, by the motion it gives to the nerves and animal spirits, conveys a certain sensation
to the mind; but it does not follow, that the sensation, motion, and resistance are any ways resembling."

occasionally used, for the same reason that the operation of bodies and the ultimate springs and principles of nature play only a silent role in his account: his concern is with what we can experience and observe. We might say Hume's interest is with the phenomena of nature (a phrase he uses), not with nature's powers. Also, of course, he was more interested in the phenomena of *human* nature than with nature at large. The phenomena of idea acquisition, of association and belief formation were what he described, rather than an attempt to characterize the nature of external objects.

He *was* interested in the nature of the object *as perceived*. Objects appear to us, we become aware of how they appear. Those appearances take the form of sense appearances of colors, shapes, sounds. These sensations, these sense impressions become transformed into ideas. To be aware of some object, e.g., a tree, we must have specific sense and ideational contents. No perceptions, no object awareness. In this way, the perceptions I have *are* the objects as they appear to us. Those objects, the objects we are aware of, the objects as known, are the very things themselves, but those objects in themselves are not dependent on appearing to perceivers. Moreover, the very objects which appear to us are the objects that are, at least in part, responsible for their appearing to us. Book II of the *Treatise* identifies three sources for original impressions, the impressions of sensation: they "arise in the soul, from the constitution of the body, from the animal spirits, or from the application of objects to the external organs" (p. 275). He characterizes these as "natural and physical causes." With this claim, we have left the domain of Hume's phenomenology, but we have not left the domain of his ontology.

It is the larger domain of nature and human nature that we need to keep in mind, if we are to appreciate the analysis Hume gives of the external objects that we know or are aware of when perceptions are present with the mind. For perceptions to be present with the mind is the same as objects appearing to us. While the ordinary view of perceptions being the very things themselves is attractive, the end of the section on skepticism and the senses reveals Hume's dissatisfaction with that view: there is, he says (on behalf of us all) an external and an internal world (*Treatise*, p. 218). Apparently, the Cartesian interpretation of the ordinary, single existence view did not, in Hume's eyes, free that account from difficulties. Probably, it was too "philosophical" or "theoretical" (despite the fact that Hume presented it as a view not burdened with theory). The trouble is, I suspect, that Hume considered that way of stating the view – the *being* of objects is in the mind in the perceptions that are intimately present to us – as a philosophical interpretation of what we all do believe. The alternative to that interpretation of the ordinary view is to try to *identify* perceptions with objects, an alternative which does seem to rule out an external world.

Quite apart from efforts to make sense of the ordinary view, there are difficulties inherent in Hume's doctrine of impressions and ideas that raise problems about talking of external objects. Given the restrictions of Hume's requirements for ideas, that they must be correlated with some impressions, the only legitimate ideas we can have of that external world have to be based on the sensations and perceptions that we experience. Just as the only legitimate idea we can have of necessary connection is the one he describes in terms of our responses to experienced constant conjunctions, so the only legitimate ideas we can have of external objects is the vulgar or ordinary view of groups of perceptions. But the story does not end there, there is more to Hume's world than our perceptions. Many philosophers refuse to allow Hume the license of accepting or believing in a world that escapes the bounds of his account of belief and meaning; they take the account of idea formation and belief acquisition offered by Hume and read that account back into the texts of those passages which seem to assume real causes and powers in nature and to accept the existence of objects that are more than perceptions. In that way, it is declared that Hume did not accept the notion of secret springs and principles and powers in nature. Those many passages that seem to assert the existence of powers in nature are thereby eliminated or rendered harmless.

There are some matters of principle in whether we can allow a philosopher to go beyond the very bounds of sense and sense-making which that philosopher advances. Without addressing that question directly, it may help to shed light on Hume's concept of the external world if we make a careful examination of those passages in the *Treatise* and the *Enquiry* which refer to secret springs and principles and to hidden powers.

7

Hume's ontology

Every thing is conducted by springs and principles . . .
Hume, *Treatise*, p. 397.

At the close of the section on personal identity in the *Treatise*, Hume distinguishes the *intellectual* world and the *natural* world (p. 263). The Appendix to this work speaks of the intellectual and material worlds (p. 633; cf. p. 232). His essay, "Of Some Remarkable Customs," refers to the moral and physical worlds.[1] The intellectual or moral world is the domain of impressions, ideas, perceptions, passions, judgment, the imagination, reason and understanding. That world also includes the perceiver, the self and the mind. It is a world which contains the principles of association, of belief formation, idea acquisition. That same intellectual and moral world contains the various items in Books II and III of the *Treatise*: emotions, moral principles, the self as moral agent.

The natural or material world is the concern of anatomy and natural philosophy (*Treatise*, p. 276). It is the world of external objects, of principles such as elasticity, gravity, or communication of motion by impulse. That world is the domain of physiology, of nerves and brain. It also seems to contain mechanisms that account for and cause the powers and operations of bodies. The phrase he uses to refer to this mechanism, "springs and principles," may suggest a mechanical concept of nature, or it just may be an analogy borrowed from machines such as clocks which were run by pulleys and springs.[2] Much of both the natural and intellectual worlds is available to experience and observation, that is the way we discover explanatory principles, if not actual operating princi-

---

[1] *Essays Moral, Political and Literary*, ed. Eugene Miller (rev. edn, Indianapolis: Liberty Fund, 1985), p. 366.
[2] There are a number of references to "machines of nature" in the *Dialogues*. The notion of the machine of the body was commonly used in the eighteenth century. For Hume's reference to the body as a "complicated machine," see his *Enquiry concerning Human Understanding*, p. 87.

ples. Experience includes, of course, observation of how we think and act, how we associate ideas, imagine events, report our intentions. The impressions and ideas that appear to us, the view or regard of ordinary objects that we have, the beliefs we form, the associations we make: all these items in the intellectual world are available to us. So are external objects available to us by means of how they appear to be. External objects belong to both worlds, to the intellectual world when they discover themselves to our senses, to the natural world in their independent existence.

I

In the last section of Book II, Part II of the *Treatise*, the section on love and hatred of animals, Hume remarks that "Every thing is conducted by springs and principles, which are not peculiar to man, or to any one species of animals." The principles here do not sound like explanatory ones; they are operating principles, principles that are responsible for the "passions of love and hatred, and . . . their mixture and composition" in man and animals. While presenting his claim that "a spectator can commonly infer our actions from our motives and character," Hume remarks that the spectator believes that where his inferences from motives and character fail, they might be successful "were he perfectly acquainted with every circumstance of our situation and temper, and the most secret springs of our complexion and disposition" (pp. 408–9). He repeats this remark verbatim in the *Enquiry concerning Human Understanding* (p. 94n). The same *Enquiry* characterizes the main use of history as the discovery of "the constant and universal principles of human nature," which it does by providing us with the information that enables us to become acquainted with "the regular springs of human action and behaviour" (p. 83). The very first section of this *Enquiry* expressed the hope that philosophy might, if conducted properly, "discover, at least in some degree, the secret springs and principles, by which the human mind is actuated in its operations" (p. 14). This remark may have been a rhetorical question with an implied negative answer. At least, such a hope is modified later when Hume affirms that the "ultimate springs and principles," the "ultimate causes of any natural operation" and the "power which produces any single effect in the universe" are "totally shut up from human curiosity and enquiry" (p. 30). He declares in the *Treatise* that "To explain the ultimate causes of our mental action is impossible" (p. 22), and later he asserts that the ultimate cause of sense impressions is inexplicable

(p. 84). No rational and modest philosopher would ever pretend to a knowledge of *ultimate* springs and principles (p. 90), but perhaps some general principles may be discovered.

No denial in this last passage that there are real causes and powers and ultimate springs at work in nature and human nature: only a denial that our knowledge can discover them. Writing about the probability of causes, and what Hume calls "the second species of probability, where there is a *contrariety* in our experience and observation" (p. 131), he remarks that the vulgar "attribute the uncertainty of events" to an uncertainty or failure in the cause to produce its usual effect. But, Hume says, "philosophers observing, that almost in every part of nature there is contain'd a vast variety of springs and principles, which are hid, by reason of their minuteness or remoteness, find that 'tis at least possible the contrariety of events may not proceed from any contingency in the cause, but from the secret operation of contrary causes" (p. 132). This passage is repeated in the *Enquiry* (p. 87).

II

Hume echoes Locke and other seventeenth-century writers in the Introduction to his *Treatise*: the essence of mind and of external objects is unknown. In Book II on the passions, he says the essence of external bodies is obscure (p. 366). He also agrees with Locke in saying it is "impossible to form any notion of its [the mind's] powers and qualities otherwise than from careful and exact experiments" (p. xvii). Hume accepted that the mind and its faculties have powers. He refers to the power of the imagination (p. 95), its powers can be disordered by "any extraordinary ferment of blood and spirits" (p. 123), and we are said to have "mental powers" (p. 180; cf. *Enquiry*, p. 14). The powers of the understanding are said to be the subject of "an exact analysis," as a way of discovering what it is fitted for (*Enquiry*, p. 12). He also refers to "an accurate scrutiny into the powers and faculties of human nature," and of a "mental geography, or delineation of the distinct parts and powers of the mind" (p. 13). In these early passages he goes on to assert firmly: "It cannot be doubted that the mind is endowed with several powers and faculties" (pp. 13–14). We are said to have natural powers which function in action (p. 45); the natural powers of the human mind are cited later (p. 63). There are a number of references to the creative power of the mind (*Enquiry*, pp. 19, 68, 69; *Treatise*, p. 84), and to the mind's power of *producing* ideas (*Treatise*, pp. 22, 60).

In these various passages from both books, Hume expresses some confidence in our ability to discover some truths about the powers and faculties of the mind and of human nature generally. He thought he had discovered some truths about the workings of the mind, of the understanding, the imagination and reason. Those powers were discovered by attending to what the faculties do and to what humans are able to do. The concept of power applied to the intellectual world refers to abilities and functions. Mental powers are our ability to reason, to imagine, to attend, to act, to love and hate, to judge. To what extent we are in control of these operations and functions may not be entirely clear from Hume's texts. The reference to "springs" suggests something other than the person is in charge. Physiology does play a determining role in some mental operations. The association of ideas, the feeling of necessity, the belief that the future will be like the past seem to occur without much if any action by us. Custom takes over. Also, that ambiguous "nature" to which Hume appeals has us under its protection, guiding our beliefs, for example, about the external world.

If the essence of the mind is unknown, we cannot say what that essence might be, but Hume manages to say rather a lot about the mind and human nature. All three books of the *Treatise* give us an elaborate and extensive description of the cognitive and emotional features of persons. The two *Enquiries*, especially the one on the principles of morals, continued that description and analysis. Hume's objective, announced in the introduction to the *Treatise*, to "explain the principles of human nature," can be said to have been fairly achieved, the science of man elaborated (p. xvi). He did not claim to have discovered ultimate, original principles, but in that respect, the science of man is no different from the other sciences (p. xviii).

III

The situation of Hume's natural or physical world is, not surprisingly, rather different. That world was the concern of physical scientists, who were at work in physics, optics and physiology, describing and offering principles applicable to physical objects and events. But Hume held some opinions about the nature of that world and our knowledge of it. Not only is the essence of body unknown, its powers are also hidden from us, experience and experiential knowledge stop at the appearances. Nevertheless, that world for Hume is a world of powers, of springs and principles that operate on and cause bodies to affect bodies, including those of perceivers. Since this claim about the physical world has been challenged recently by philosophers who say (a) it is not Hume's view, but the view of others, or (b) it should not be Hume's view, we need to proceed cautiously. Can we hear Hume's voice in some of the passages that speak of secret springs and principles, and hidden powers in nature?

Some of the passages do report what others say or believe. For example, reporting on modern philosophy, Hume refers to the theory that all the growth and changes in animals and plants, and the operation of bodies on each other "are nothing but changes of figure and motion," a reference to the corpuscular theory accepted by many scientists and philosophers (*Treatise*, p. 227). In addition, the claim was that there are no other principles in "the material universe," at least no other principles of which we can form an idea. Hume indicates that he has many objections to this theory (he says "system"), but the one he cites here is that the theory leads to skepticism about the external world since it turns secondary qualities into mere perceptions (p. 228). He does not reject the notion of "elements and powers of nature" (p. 227). That phrase is also found in Book II, Part II, section V (p. 363) and in Book II, Part III, section I (p. 401). In the latter section, he also refers to "the cohesion of the parts of matter," cohesion being due to "natural and necessary principles." References to cohesion and particles are found elsewhere as well.[3] So there are some ingredients of the corpuscular theory in Hume's account. A passage in the *Enquiry concerning Human Understanding* repeats a modified version of the remark I cited from pp. 131–2 of the *Treatise* about unusual or unexpected events: "The generality of mankind never find any difficulty in accounting for the more common and familiar operations of nature," but when confronted with extraordinary events, the generality of mankind tend to look for "some invisible intelligent principle," rather than to "the common powers of nature" (p. 69). Whether those common powers are a function of the cohesion of particles, Hume does not say, but the contrast with "intelligent principle" suggests that he favors the more mechanical features of matter. Intelligent principles of the sort invoked by Malebranche, the power of God or other spirits to cause events in nature, are unacceptable for Hume, but the powers that he seems to accept are not intelligible (i.e., they lack meaning); they escape our experience and understanding.[4]

---

[3] For example, see *Treatise*, pp. 221, 227, 399.

[4] For Hume's reference to the "intelligent principle" of Malebranche in the *Treatise*, see pp. 159–60. He says this opinion is "very curious."

The contrast between intelligent principles and the common powers of nature is important for Hume; it is a contrast that he makes much of in the *Natural History of Religion*. He rejects the former and accepts the latter, even though the common powers of nature may be difficult to understand. Philosophers "perceive that, even in the most familiar events, the energy of the cause is as unintelligible as in the most unusual, and that we only learn by experience the frequent *Conjunction* of objects, without being ever able to comprehend anything like the *Connexion* between them" (p. 70). He does not reject the notion of powers in nature, he simply explains how most people and philosophers deal with the events they experience: most people accept causal powers as accounting for events, philosophers say the powers of nature are unintelligible. In a later passage, Hume says that, even recognizing the limitations of our knowledge to experience, "men still entertain a strong propensity to believe that they penetrate farther into the powers of nature, and perceive something like a necessary connexion between the cause and the effect" (*Enquiry*, p. 92). No rejection by Hume of real necessary connections in nature, only a disclaimer that we can discover such connections.

There are two other passages in the *Treatise* that refer to powers of objects. His argument in the first passage addresses the claim that *reason* can infer or conclude, from an experience of constant conjunction of events, that powers of production are involved. The claim of those who give reason that task say "there is a just foundation for drawing a conclusion from the existence of one object to that of its usual attendant" (p. 90). Even allowing the assumption that "the production of one object by another in any one instance implies a power; and that this power is connected to the effect," Hume responded that no proof (or reason) can be given why the same power "is always conjoin'd with like sensible qualities" (p. 91). The stress is on what reason can or cannot do. Hume's conclusion is that "not only our reason fails us in the discovery of the *ultimate connexion* of causes and effects, but even after experience has informed us of their *constant conjunction*, 'tis impossible for us to satisfy ourselves by our reason, why we shou'd extend that experience beyond those particular instances, which have fallen under our observation" (p. 91). We cannot reason to the existence of powers in bodies.[5]

---

[5] There is an interesting, brief reference to reason in Book III of the *Treatise*. He argues there that reason is inactive in relation to action, but he speaks of reason exerting itself in both natural and moral subjects, "whether it considers the power of external bodies, or the actions of rational beings" (p. 457). He does not say what the considering by reason of the powers of bodies amounts to or involves. Does it consider whether there are powers in bodies, or is Hume assuming that there are such powers and that reason thinks about them?

The second passage deals with belief, the causes of belief. His account is summed up as follows: "There enters nothing into the operation of the mind but a present impression, a lively idea, and a relation or association in fancy betwixt the impression and the idea" (p. 101). He considers an alternate claim. Suppose, he says, "there is an object presented, from which I draw a certain conclusion, and form to myself ideas, which I am said to believe or assent to" (p. 102). If it be thought that the objects "influence each other by their particular powers and qualities," my belief cannot be caused by those powers and qualities because they are "entirely unknown." Granted that this example is a supposition by Hume to reinforce his identification of the causes of belief as the present impression and some action by the imagination, his point is not that there are no powers in objects, but that if there are powers, they could not be the cause of our belief.

There are two passages in the *Enquiry* which draw the same limitation to reason as the *Treatise* passage above. He makes the point that "even after we have experiences of the operation of cause and effect, our conclusions from such experiences are not founded on reasoning, or on any process of the understanding" (p. 32). What follows seems clearly to be Hume's firm opinion: "It must certainly be allowed, that nature has kept us at a great distance from all her secrets, and has afforded us only the knowledge of a few superficial qualities of objects; while she conceals from us those powers and principles on which the influence of objects entirely depends" (pp. 32–3). Our various senses provide information about qualities such as color, weight or the motion of bodies, but we do not discover (and reason is no help either), e.g., what makes bread nourish us, or what is the "wonderful force or powers" which move bodies (p. 33). We are ignorant of those "natural powers and principles" which we all presume do exist. Everyone agrees, Hume says, that "there is no known connexion between the sensible qualities and the secret powers," so the conclusions we form about the future being like the past (e.g., that the next piece of bread will also nourish) are not based on a knowledge of those powers.

He offers the same claim in a passage a few pages later with the example of a person with "strong faculties of reason and reflection," who is "brought on a sudden into the world" (p. 42). Such a person would be unable to form by reason the idea of cause and effect from observing the "continual succession of objects." He would be unable to do so because "the particular powers by which all natural operations are performed, never appear to the senses" (p. 42). The *Abstract* makes the same

point. "Were a man, such as *Adam*, created in the full vigour of understanding, without experience, he would never be able to infer motion in
the second ball from the motion and impulse of the first. It is not any
thing that reason sees in the cause, which makes us *infer* the effect" (p.
650).[6] In the *Treatise*, Hume offers several examples of the way we anticipate similar events from past experiences, remarking that there "is a
kind of pre-established harmony between the course of nature and the
succession of our ideas; and though the powers and forces, by which the
former is governed, be wholly unknown by us; yet our thoughts and con-
ceptions have still, we find, gone on in the same train with the other
works of nature" (pp. 54–5). He identifies nature as the source of the
instinct we have "which carries forward the thought in a correspondent
course to that which she has established among external objects; though
we are ignorant of those powers and forces, on which this regular course
and succession of objects totally depends" (p. 55). A *total* dependence on
powers and forces: an unequivocal affirmation!

IV

There is a footnote on p. 33 of the *Enquiry*, the passage cited above about
our ignorance of natural powers, which needs attention. The note is
about the term "powers." "The word Power, is here used in a loose and
popular sense. The more accurate explication of it would give additional
evidence to this argument. See Sect. 7." In that section, he speaks of
"that vulgar inaccurate idea" of power (p. 67n). He also says of the words
"force," "power" and "energy" that as "commonly used, [they] have
very loose meanings annexed to them; and their ideas are very uncertain
and confused" (p. 77n). It may be important that he does not say the
vulgar, common use of these terms is without meaning, but I will return
to that question of meaning later. For now, we need to remind ourselves
of the *argument* for which the accurate use of "power" gives additional
evidence and support. The argument or claim is that our confidence in
future events being like past events is founded on custom and experience,
not on inferences of reason. So the accurate explication of "power" (that
it is a feeling we have under certain conditions) reinforces this claim: our
confidence is not based on a knowledge of natural powers.

---

[6] Cf. *Enquiry concerning Human Understanding*, p. 27: "Adam, though his rational faculties be supposed,
at the very first, entirely perfect, could not have inferred from the fluidity and transparency of
water that it would suffocate him, or from the light and warmth of fire that it would consume
him."

He reiterates this claim several times in section VII (pp. 73, 74). There he also explains what it would be like did we have a knowledge of the natural powers of objects. "From the appearance of an object, we never can conjecture what effect will result from it. But were the power or energy of any cause discoverable by the mind, we could foresee the effect, even without experience; and might, at first, pronounce with certainty concerning it, by the mere dint of thought and reasoning" (p. 63; see also pp. 66, 67). A similar remark is found in the *Abstract*, with the example of Adam, rather than just a person "brought on a sudden into the world." If Adam were able to infer the motion of the second billiard ball from that of the first, without any prior experience, such an inference "would amount to a demonstration, as being founded merely on the comparison of ideas" (p. 650).[7] Hume makes this same point about the claim that we are aware of power in volition, in moving our limbs. "But if by consciousness we perceived any power or energy in the will, we must know its power; we must know its connexion with the effect; we must know the secret union of soul and body, and the nature of both these substances; by which the one is able to operate, in so many instances, upon the other" (*Enquiry*, p. 65). To be conscious of the power of the will, "We should then perceive, independent of experience, why the authority of will over the organs of the body is circumscribed within such particular areas" (p. 65). Instead, "We learn the influence of our will from experience alone" (p. 66). A few pages earlier he said "The influence, we may observe, is a fact, which, like all other natural events, can be known only by experience, and can never be foreseen from any apparent energy or power in the cause, which connects it with the effect" (pp. 64–5).[8]

The language of influence continues to be used in his section on liberty and necessity. Not every occurrence expresses Hume's own view. For example, the vulgar are said to believe a cause has lost its usual influence, when unexpected results occur (p. 86), or an artisan "easily

---

[7] The *Treatise* makes the same point. "Now nothing is more evident, than that the human mind cannot form such an idea of two objects, as to conceive any connexion betwixt them, or comprehend distinctly that power or efficacy, by which they are united. Such a connexion wou'd amount to a demonstration, and wou'd imply the absolute impossibility for the one object not to follow, or to be conceiv'd not to follow upon the other" (pp. 161–2). Hume is repeating a claim Locke took some pains to make: a knowledge of real essence would give us a knowledge of effects without trial or experience. See for example *Essay*, 2.31.6 and 4.3.25. For some discussion of this claim by Locke, see my *Locke and the Compass of Human Understanding*, pp. 82–5.

[8] For the corresponding argument in the *Treatise*, see p. 632, his insert for p. 161.

perceives that the same force on the springs and pendulum has always the same influence on its wheels" (p. 87). But in making his case for the uniformity of human behavior, Hume speaks in his own voice: motives "have a regular and uniform influence on the Mind" (p. 98), or "the same motives always produce the same actions" (p. 83). Characters of specific sorts "have a determinate power to produce particular sentiments" (p. 90). Liberty is even defined in power terms: "By liberty, then, we can only mean *a power of acting or not acting, according to the determination of the will*" (p. 95). The corresponding section on liberty and necessity in Book II of the *Treatise*, some of which the *Enquiry* section repeats, carries these same words. The stress is upon the uniform and regular relation between motives and actions; those uniformities influence our understanding and determine us "to infer to the existence of the one from that of the other" (*Treatise*, p. 404). Reason is denied to have an influence on the will, but passions do (p. 415).

Hume's intention in these discussions of liberty and necessity was to show that there is a similar "necessity" (i.e., uniformity) in the physical and moral domains. Just as we discover regular sequences in physical events, so in human action we can discover the constancy of specific passions and motives with certain judgments and actions. In both domains, we learn to anticipate and predict. So we can ask: why does Hume resort to terms such as "influence," "produce" and "arise from"? It may be thought that these terms are just a shorthand for a longer, more cumbersome locution. In saying, for example, that we learn the *influence* of the will, Hume may only be saying that we learn some events such as that a leg or arm moves when we want to walk or wave, perhaps a translation from the inaccurate vulgar language into the accurate language of the strict use of power terms.[9] But before we succumb to that tempting suggestion, we need to notice a number of passages in section VII of the *Enquiry* which seem to be positive and forthright in the use of power language.

(1) Pages 63–4: "The scenes of the universe are continually shifting, and one object follows another in an uninterrupted succession; but the power or force, which actuates the whole machine [of nature], is

---

[9] "Influence" is a term Hume also uses in Book II of the *Treatise* about external objects. "It has been observ'd already, that in no single instance the ultimate connexion of any objects is discoverable, either by the senses or reason, and that we can never penetrate so far into the essence and construction of bodies, as to perceive the principle, on which their mutual influence depends" (Book II, Part III, section I, p. 400). This passage is quoted in the *Abstract*, p. 660.

entirely concealed from us, and never discovers itself in any of the sensible qualities of body."[10]

(2) Page 65: "The motion of our body follows upon the command of our will. Of this we are every moment conscious. But the means, by which this is effected; the energy, by which the will performs so extraordinary an operation; of this we are so far from being immediately conscious, that it must for ever escape our most diligent enquiry."

(3) Page 66: Experience "only teaches us, how one event constantly follows another; without instructing us in the secret connexion, which binds them together, and renders them inseparable."

(4) Page 67: The "power or energy by which this [motion of limbs], is effected like that of other natural events, is unknown and inconceivable."

(5) Page 68: "We only feel the event, namely, the existence of an idea, consequent to a command of the will: But the manner, in which this operation is performed, the power by which it is produced, is entirely beyond our comprehension."

(6) Page 70: Philosophers are said to discover that, "as we are totally ignorant of the power on which depends the mutual operation of bodies, we are no less ignorant of that power on which depends the operation of mind on body, of body on mind."

(7) Page 71: Objecting to those philosophers (he must have Malebranche in mind) who make God the cause of all action, including our action of moving limbs, Hume remarks: "They rob nature, and all created beings, of every power, in order to render their dependence on the Deity still more sensible and immediate."[11]

---

[10] Kenneth P. Winkler ("The New Hume," *The Philosophical Review*, 100, no. 4, October 1991, 549), says about this passage that "the whole machine" refers to "the world *in so far as we observe it*, the shifting scenes we *sense*." This is a rather dubious interpretation. Hume's paragraph on p. 63 begins by saying "no part of matter, that does ever, by its sensible qualities, discover any force or energy." Winkler apparently takes the phrase "its sensible qualities" to identify matter's *only* qualities. Of course our acquaintance with the machine of nature can only be with its sensible qualities, but I see no reason to support the suggestion that Hume limited nature to what we sense. In his extended discussion of the idea of necessary connection (Book I, Part III, section XIV) Hume argues that there are no *known* qualities of matter which supply us with the idea of power. "Known" qualities do not, I think, exhaust the qualities of matter.

[11] It is relevant to note that, in a long footnote at the end of his discussion of that Malebranchian theory, Hume remarks that "It was never the meaning of Sir Isaac Newton to rob second causes of all power or energy" (p. 73n). He also reminds us that Locke, Clarke and Cudworth supposed "that matter has a real, though subordinate and derived power." When in the Appendix to the *Treatise* he says "matter is confess'd by philosophers [natural philosophers, scientists] to operate by an unknown power," he probably had Newtonians in mind (p. 633).

(8) Page 72: "We are ignorant, it is true, of the manner in which bodies operate on each other: Their force or energy is entirely incomprehensible."

Besides "power" and "energy" the words to notice in these passages (words that occur throughout both the *Enquiry* and the *Treatise*) are: "actuates" in 1; "effected" in 2; "produced" in 5; and "operates" in 8. These words all indicate actions, not just sequences, of bodies and minds. Hume recognized that these terms are alternate (he says, synonymous) words for "cause": "Thus, if cause be defined, *that which produces any thing*; it is easy to observe, that *producing* is synonimous to *causing*" (*Enquiry*, p. 96n). The *Treatise* gives other synonyms, such as "efficacy," "agency," "power" and "force" (p. 157). His remark in the *Enquiry* footnote is meant to forestall someone thinking that Hume's definition of "cause" can be circumvented by using a word such as "produce." The implication of Hume's remark is that all those synonyms should be defined as he does "cause," in terms of regular sequences of events. What is interesting about the *Enquiry* passage is the way Hume himself switches from "cause" to "produce": "Had no objects a regular conjunction with each other, we should never have entertained any notion of cause and effect; and this regular conjunction produces that inference of the understanding . . ." To produce an inference sounds as if he is saying the regular conjunction of events is not just followed by our inference, but the sequence (and now we have to use one of Hume's power words) "produces," "gives rise to," "actuates" the inference. Throughout both books, events and processes in nature are actuated, limbs are moved, ideas produced,[12] bodies operate on other bodies[13] and on minds, minds act on the body and its animal spirits. All we can discover by experience is the sequencing of objects and events.

With these passages in front of us, and keeping in mind the many other references to powers in nature in the *Treatise* and the *Enquiry*, it is difficult not to reach the conclusion that despite our ignorance, Hume had no doubts about the existence of such powers, springs and principles. He says not only that we do not have any knowledge of them, but that they are incomprehensible, unintelligible and, his most telling

---

[12] The phrase "arise from," sometimes used by Hume, also indicates action. Hume offers three possible sources for the production of impressions from the senses, the source from which they arise: "immediately from the object, or [they] are produc'd by the creative power of the mind, or are derived from the author of our being" (*Treatise*, p. 84). These sources correspond to Descartes's adventitious, factitious and innate ideas.

[13] See *Treatise*, p. 399 where he refers to "the operations of external bodies" and "the communication of their motion, their attraction, and natural cohesion."

phrase, "these words [connection and power] are absolutely without any meaning" (*Enquiry*, p. 74, see also p. 96 for "unintelligible terms"). His despairing Conclusion to Book 1 is equally emphatic: "it appears, that when we say we desire to know the ultimate and operating principle, as something, which resides in the external object, we either contradict ourselves or talk without a meaning" (p. 267). Does the word "appears" suggest some modification of the strong statement in the *Enquiry*? The *Abstract* is not quite so harsh as the *Enquiry*: "Upon the whole, then, either we have no idea at all of force or energy, and the words are altogether insignificant, or they can mean nothing but that determination of the thought, acquir'd by habit, to pass from the cause to its usual effect" (p. 657).[14] The meaninglessness is said to apply to philosophical reasoning about powers, as well as to the use of the term in common life.[15] The loose and inaccurate vulgar sense of "power" turns out to have no sense, no meaning, not just a loose sense! The only way the terms "force," "energy" and "power" can acquire a meaning, the only legitimate idea we can form of power is found in the "accurate explication" of it: one object followed by another and the anticipation of similar sequences in the future (*Enquiry*, pp. 76–7). To say that Hume accepts the existence of real causes, natural powers that operate on bodies and produce effects, while at the same time insisting that the idea of natural powers is without any meaning, would seem to place Hume in an absurd position. It would seem to imply that his careful account of idea acquisition and belief-formation does not apply to his larger view of the physical world. Nothing that Hume has said explicitly allows such an exception in our ideas or beliefs.

v

Kenneth Winkler is convinced that Hume intended his theory of ideas to apply to "every conception or supposition."[16] This means, he says,

---

[14] He adds an intriguing comment two sentences later, advising the reader to consult the author, i.e., the *Treatise* itself. He says it is sufficient here if "I can make the learned world apprehend, that there is some difficulty in the case, and that who-ever solves the difficulty must say something very new and extraordinary; as new as the difficulty itself." It is not clear what difficulty he refers to. Could it have something to do with the two uses of "power," the loose, inaccurate and the accurate use?

[15] Cf. *Treatise*, p. 162: "when we talk of a superior or inferior nature, as endow'd with a power or force, proportion'd to any effect; when we speak of a necessary connexion betwixt objects, and suppose, that this connexion depends upon an efficacy or energy, with which any of these objects are endow'd; in all these expressions, *so apply'd*, we have really no distinct meaning, and make use only of common words, without any clear and determinate ideas."

[16] Winkler, "The New Hume," p. 560.

that "Every thought or perception must be derived from impressions." Any thought or idea "whose derivation fails to satisfy" that condition, or which is not a result of some action of the mind (e.g., compounding, mixing) "is not a thought or perception at all." With one exception, Hume does not say we have an idea of the power of objects; that exception speaks of an inaccurate idea of power.[17] From his principle that "all ideas are deriv'd from impressions, or some precedent *perceptions*," Hume draws the obvious conclusion, "'tis impossible we can have any idea of power and efficacy, unless some instances can be produc'd, wherein this power *is perceiv'd to exert itself*" (*Treatise*, p. 160). The only legitimate idea we can have of power is the one he identifies from the constant conjunctions and internal feeling of constraint that we experience. So we need to ask: can Hume accept the existence of natural powers and real connections in nature without having an idea of them? If the very words he uses are without any meaning, there seems to be no room for what I have called his larger world, the world that is not experienced. There may be no room either for a "supposition" or a "presumption," two words used by Hume, about secret springs and powers: we cannot suppose what we cannot understand, what is incomprehensible.

We might think that the reference to a loose, vulgar meaning of the term "power" (in the footnotes on pp. 33 and 67 of the *Enquiry*) provides Hume with some wiggle-room, although the idea of power there is characterized as an inaccurate one. Section VII also speaks of that *idea* as inaccurate and confused. Do confused ideas (or confused thoughts) fall between meaningless ones and those that meet the criterion of derivation from impressions? Locke spends time describing confused ideas, but there does not seem to be such a category or class of ideas for Hume. He does credit some of the claims about liberty and necessity in human action to "confus'd ideas and undefin'd terms, which we commonly make use of in our reasonings" (*Treatise*, p. 404). Much earlier he says that "many of our ideas are so obscure, that 'tis almost impossible ever for the mind, which forms them, to tell exactly their nature and composition" (p. 33).[18] Later in the *Treatise* he criticizes those philosophers who talk of abstract ideas as pure and intellectual: "'Tis easy to see, why philosophers are so fond of this notion of some spiritual and refin'd

---

[17] *Enquiry concerning Human Understanding*, p. 67n. In that note, Hume refers to the "sentiment of an endeavour" which we feel in trying to "overcome resistance" (think of Locke's football). While there is "no known connexion" of that feeling with any event, Hume admits "that the animal *nisus* which we experience, though it can afford no accurate precise idea of power, enters very much into that vulgar inaccurate idea, which is formed of it."

[18] He quotes this remark in his *Abstract*, p. 648.

perceptions; since by that means they cover many of their absurdities, and may refuse to submit to the decisions of clear ideas, by appealing to such as are obscure and uncertain" (p. 72). General ideas are more obscure than other ideas (p. 425). Ideas that are derived from impressions are "clear and precise." Can there be loose meanings as well as "tight" or "clear" meanings, or are the footnotes on p. 33 and 67 about loose meanings simply Hume's way of leading us to a firm rejection of such meaning?

Winkler's analysis of the footnote on p. 33 is interesting for what it does not analyze. He does not mention the argument that Hume offers for the claim that reason cannot infer from appearances to powers or to effects. What Winkler stresses is the accurate idea of power in section VII, insisting that "Retrospective interpretation" of earlier inaccurate uses of "power" in terms of the accurate one "is exactly what Hume expects us to do" (p. 544). So the many assertions of hidden powers in the *Enquiry* and the *Treatise* are to be rewritten, replacing that term with the accurate one of conjunctions. Winkler offers some examples of such a rewriting for passages in the *Enquiry*. He claims that when Hume says on p. 55 that we are ignorant of powers and forces on which the regular course of nature depends, that can be rewritten as "we are ignorant of certain *objects* whose behavior is constantly conjoined with the behavior of the objects we observe" (p. 547). Strangely, Winkler retains the term "actuated" in his explication, placing the word in quotation marks: "The objects we observe are 'actuated' by those unobserved objects" (p. 547). Does he mean for us to rewrite "actuated" in terms of other objects? I take that term to be an action word, even a power word: if something actuates something else, it brings it about. The unknown objects which Winkler wants to say actuate the observed ones are, he suggests, "the parts and particles of eighteenth-century natural philosophy" (p. 548).[19] He cites a passage from Hume's *Natural History of Religion* which, he thinks, supports the suggested rewrite. Notice the terms "machinery" and "produced" in this passage: "could men anatomize nature, according to the most probable, at least the most intelligible philosophy, they would find, that these causes are nothing but the particular fabric and

---

[19] I assume Winkler is referring to the corpuscular theory which had insensible particles or corpuscles as causal agents of matter, affecting physical objects and perceivers. Apparently, Winkler is suggesting that Hume could reformulate that theory in terms of constant conjunctions of extended, moving particles and changes in the qualities of objects and in the sensations of perceivers. I am suggesting that what Hume was doing with his many references to powers and springs was reflecting the growing eighteenth-century replacement of corpuscular matter with matter that was mainly force and power.

structure of the minute parts of their own bodies and of external objects; and that, by a regular and constant machinery, all the events are produced."[20] This passage in the *Natural History of Religion* opens with the clear assertion that "We are placed in this world, as in a great theatre, where the true springs and causes of every event are entirely concealed from us." Hume goes on to remark that "We hang in perpetual suspense between life and death, health and sickness, plenty and want." These are "distributed amongst the human species by secret and unknown causes, whose operation is oft unexpected, and always unaccountable." People worry about these "unknown powers" on which we depend; we use our imagination to try to form ideas of those forces. As a result, men tend to think of those powers in a vague and general way, but usually crediting them to intelligent agents. Hume's alternative to intelligent agents is, as this passage makes clear, the structure and parts of matter. Winkler ignores the earlier sentences in this section (§III) and seems to miss the point Hume is making. There are unknown causes at work but they are mechanical and physical, not spiritual or intelligent.

If, as Winkler wants to say, powers are just unknown *objects*, those objects in this passage from Hume play a productive role in the observed and known world. Just how the machinery works to produce events Winkler leaves unexplained. He offers no account of how the unknown powers and machinery produce effects, but they would seem not to be just unknown objects, they would have to be unknown objects that *produce* results in the observed world of appearances, that is, unknown objects with powers of production. Or does Winkler intend to replace a word such as "produced" with the phrase "constantly conjoined"? He cites this passage from Hume in support of his suggested rewrite, but I would think he would have to eliminate the term "produced," and he would need to rewrite this passage as well.[21] There are many occurrences of that word in Books II and III of the *Treatise* when Hume discusses human action. Emotions and motives produce actions, objects excite passions. The implied program in Winkler's suggestion for replacing power words and, I would think, words such as "produce" and "excite," would require a major rewriting of Hume's books. That rewriting would not just be retrospective from the point where Hume presents his accurate idea of power; it would have to extend beyond that point in

---

[20] Winkler, "The New Hume," p. 548, quoted from *Works*, ed. Green and Grose, 4: 316.

[21] The word "produce" occurs late in the *Treatise* also. For example, "Like causes still produce like effects; in the same manner as in the natural action of the elements and powers of nature" (Book II, Part III, section I, p. 401).

Book I of the *Treatise*, into Books II and III. I do not suppose Winkler is really recommending rewriting Hume, replacing loose, inaccurate words with accurate ones, replacing our ordinary way of talking with Hume's experiential, justified language. But if not, Hume would still be left with the embarrassment of unintelligible and meaningless terms at least in his account of the natural world.[22]

VI

Winkler mentions, in a kind of tangential way, Hume's account in the *Enquiry* of what it would be like were we able to know the hidden powers of nature, namely, that we would know without experience what effects would follow. "Let us suppose," Winkler suggests, "that the secret springs are not objective powers or connections but objects . . . In that case, Hume is saying that the power we attribute to secret springs is nothing over and above our tendency (a hypothetical tendency in this case) to infer certain effects from objects yet unknown. To say that there are secret powers is to say that *were we acquainted with these unknown objects and their patterns of behavior*, we could predict the future with greater reliability" (p. 577). But "greater reliability" is too weak for the claim that Hume (following Locke) makes: Hume says, as we saw above, we would *know* the "connexions" between cause and effect, we would perceive (understand) how the will moves limbs.

Hume, along with Locke, wanted to explain that, if we had a knowledge of real causes in nature, of powers and necessary connections between physical objects (matter), we would have an *a priori*, demonstrative science of nature. The alternative is an experiential science of nature. The fact that we cannot predict the behavior of objects, even with probability, until we have a fund of experience of the uniformity of events, is evidence enough that we do not have the tools or the information for an *a priori* science. From this fact, can we say that Hume (or

---

[22] In his detailed study of Hume (*Cognition and Commitment in Hume's Philosophy*, New York: Oxford University Press, 1997), Don Garrett has two brief sections towards the end of his book carrying the headings: "The Inconceivability of Real Causal Connections" and "The Illusion of Ultimate Causal Principles" (pp. 220–2). Earlier, Garrett admits that "It is true, however, that for Hume there is no contradiction in the general supposition that there are things or qualities (nature unspecifiable) that we cannot represent" (p. 114). He says of Winkler that he "has argued convincingly that none of Hume's remarks commit him to that view [that there is something unrepresentable], and that Hume's position is, as it should be, skeptical or agnostic about the existence of unrepresentable and hence inconceivable objects and qualities." (*Ibid.*)

Locke) rejected the notion of necessary connection, of powers in matter? Hume does say "It is universally allowed that matter, in all its operations, is actuated by a necessary force, and that every natural effect is so precisely determined by the energy of the cause that no other effect, in such particular circumstances, could possibly have resulted from it" (*Enquiry*, p. 82). The corresponding *Treatise* passage speaks of "fate": "Every object is determin'd by an absolute fate to a certain degree and direction of its motion, and can no more depart from that precise line, in which it moves, than it can convert itself into an angel, or spirit, or any superior substance. The actions, therefore, of matter are to be regarded as instances of necessary actions" (p. 400). Whether Hume agrees with what is universally allowed, perhaps we cannot say with confidence. The notion of necessity in matter is important for his argument on liberty and necessity in human action. However, Hume is careful to explain that he is using the term "necessity" in his sense of either a constant conjunction or the inference we make when confronted with regular conjunctions of events (p. 409). Anyone who disagrees with him may refuse to call the conjunctions and inference "necessity," or such a person might "maintain there is something else in the operations of matter" (p. 410). Hume says he may be wrong in "asserting that we have no idea of any other connexion in the actions of body." The dispute does not seem to be over the question of whether matter has other properties (powers or real necessary connections). The question is about our *idea* of matter.

The issue is of some importance, since Hume is calling attention to what he takes to be a similarity between the action of bodies and the actions of persons. The ascription of necessity to the latter would be seen as ruling out free will. If the actions of matter are controlled by "fate" or necessary connections, there is no room for any deviations, unless another cause intervenes. With such a concept of necessity, Hume would have been faced with the puzzle Kant addressed: how is freedom of human action possible in a world governed by causal determinism? Hume neatly side-steps that puzzle, in effect, by redefining matter, or limiting our concept of matter to what we can discover by experience.

I do not ascribe to the will that unintelligible necessity, which is suppos'd to lie in matter. But I ascribe to matter, that intelligible quality, call it necessity or not, which the most rigorous orthodoxy does or must allow to belong to the will. I change, therefore, nothing in the receiv'd systems, with regard to the will, but only with regard to material objects. (p. 410)

Material objects are now the objects of experience, objects whose qualities and uniformities we rely on in everyday experience. Objects in this sense have no hidden powers; they are just as we perceive them to be. The system of perceived objects and the system of human actions are similar in respect to their uniformities and predictabilities.

I have characterized the redefinition of matter as side-stepping the puzzle made famous by Kant: how can free human action exist (coexist) in a natural, physical world of causal determination? Such a charge of side-stepping that question can be leveled against Hume only if we take him to be serious in (a) his many assertions of real causes and powers in nature and (b) his clear account of what a knowledge of such powers and causes would yield: an *a priori* science of nature. I take Hume to be serious about (a) and (b); he speaks in his own voice in those many passages. Kant was quite explicit in affirming that the system of nature is determined; each event is determined by a predecessor event, a determination which would seem to make it impossible for the system of human action to find a purchase in the physical world, the very world where our actions clearly take place. Kant was content to offer concepts of free causality and absolute beginnings of events, thereby opening the way for conceiving of the possibility of moral actions in a fully determined world. Hume's redefinition of matter, his limiting what we can say about material objects to what we can learn through experience and observation, takes the determination out of the world. He is left with a world of uniformities and constant conjunctions. The system of human action is then shown to have the same characteristics.

It was important for Hume to make the point that there are uniformities in human actions, regular conjunctions of motives, circumstances and volitions. Nature and human nature do not differ in this respect. It was also important for him to remind his readers that he has shown in Book I that we do not have a clear or even an intelligible idea of those hidden powers, the secret springs and principles at work in the material universe. The "unintelligible necessity" has been replaced by the "intelligible quality" of predictability and a feeling of necessity when we are confronted with regular successions of events. In the passage from Book II, p. 410 of the *Treatise*, there is no assertion of hidden powers, but he does allow, as we saw, that he may be mistaken in saying we have no idea of such powers. His concern is to emphasize what he is not ascribing to the will: a blind, fateful necessity. But equally, there is nothing incompatible between this passage and those many references to and assertions of powers and forces in objects, found throughout the *Treatise* and the

Enquiry, and one or two references in the *Abstract*. So I think it is very difficult to deny that Hume recognized powers in physical nature, in the material world.

In the end, we may just have to accept the fact that there is in Hume's writings a combination of ordinary language and the more specialized language based on his theory of ideas and belief. Hume clearly did not want to abandon our ordinary way of speaking or thinking, but he was frustrated at his inability to find a way to defend the ordinary terms used in referring to physical objects, their powers, their operating principles, their independent existence. That is one of his laments in his famous melancholic Conclusion to Book I of the *Treatise*. He regrets that reason, on his analysis, is unable to supply him with a concept of object that applies to more than perceptions of the present moment. Experience and habit do "enliven some ideas beyond others," but they give us no basis for attributing any existence "but what was dependent upon the senses; and must comprehend them entirely in that succession of perceptions, which constitutes our self or person" (p. 265). He was hoping for some argument which could keep objects close to perceptions and appearances while still granting those objects an independent status. Within the confines of his theory of ideas (they must be derived from impressions), his hoped-for defence of object realism escapes his system. In this respect, he ends up in the predicament he voiced at the end of the section on modern philosophy:

Thus there is a direct and total opposition betwixt our reason and our senses; or more properly speaking, betwixt those conclusions we form from cause and effect, and those that persuade us of the continu'd and independent existence of body. When we reason from cause and effect, we conclude, that neither colour, sound, taste, nor smell have a continu'd and independent existence. When we exclude these sensible qualities there remains nothing in the universe, which has such an existence. (p. 231)

The failure to find grounds for a realism of objects was not the only failure Hume recognized in that Conclusion to Book I, although it is the first one mentioned there. The next failure he mentions concerns our desire to penetrate to ultimate principles. "We would not willingly stop before we are acquainted with that energy in the cause, by which it operates on its effect; that tie, which connects them together; and that efficacious quality, on which the tie depends. This is our aim in all our studies and reflections" (p. 266). Such a clear statement of his goal, his hopes, proves impossible of attainment, perhaps it is even meaningless. His method of impressions-ideas does not lead to the conclusion that there are no independent objects, operating principles or powers in objects. The safe course to take is to characterize Hume's position as that of skeptical realism, as John Wright has done.[23] I am tempted to be more bold and say that Hume "believed" that there is a material world of independently existing objects with forces and powers, real "causes." I have to place "believed" and "causes" in quotation marks because Hume's methodology has usurped those words and given them a technical, restricted meaning. Put more succinctly, I would say Hume's ontology includes these items, an independent material world of forces and powers. He clearly did not want to deny that ontology, that is why he agonized so forlornly in the Conclusion to Book I. Had he been convinced by his reasoning that objects are only perceptions, that power is only a term applied to sequences of events and our feelings, the concerns he expresses in that Conclusion would have been unnecessary, they would have been dissolved.

---

[23] See his *The Sceptical Realism of David Hume* (Manchester: Manchester University Press, 1983). See also Galen Strawson, *The Secret Connexion: Causation, Realism and David Hume* (Oxford: Clarendon Press, 1989).

The realism of appearances

Astronomers are more apt to look at their telescope's monitors than to consider the stars with their naked eyes. But we continue to use our senses to interpret the work of the computers, to see the monitors, to judge and analyze, and to design ever newer dreams of artificial intelligence. Never will we leave the palace of our perceptions.

Diane Ackerman, Natural History of the Senses (1990), p. 301

Suppose then a hollow Globe with Perception, and painted on the Inside with Birds, Beasts and Fishes, and to have the knowledge of all that is delineated within it; the whole Delineation being within the Globe, and the Perception the Globe hath of it but one Act, is it not certain that the Appearance which this Representation would most naturally make to the Globe must be of something comprehended within it self? And the same it would probably be with the Mind, if there were not some external world, to signify and represent which our Ideas, by the Rules of divine Perspective, appear External.

Henry Grove, An Essay Towards a Demonstration of the Soul's Immateriality
(1718), pp. 16–17

Surely, any modern direct-realist theory of perception will allow causal intermediaries between object and percipient: no one would dream of denying the title of direct realism to a theory of perception merely because it tolerates causal intermediaries.

Robert Pasnau, Theories of Cognition in the Later Middle Ages (1997), p. 300

Each of these quotations relates to a key topic or issue embedded in those categories or contrasts listed in the Introduction. Diane Ackerman reminds us of an obvious fact, that our access to the world (to the physical world at least) is through perception. Churchland seems to overlook this fact in his claim that a neuroscientist, lacking the ability to see color, could know what it is like to see red just by consulting the dials of a machine. Churchland ignored the fact that Mary was using sense qualia when she looked at the machine's recording of information about brain activity. The *experience* of seeing red, as for any experience of any sense modality, is not the same as the neural processes that are part causes of those qualia. Perceptions and appearances are what we have to work with.

Henry Grove, with his charming, percipient, painted globe presents us with a graphic analogy of the mind and its ideas, where ideas are the objects of the mind's perception and awareness. Grove believed that even were there no external world, we might have the perceptual experiences we have, for Grove because God could so arrange it. Grove's globe can be seen as a *reductio*, in the service of skepticism, a warning that if ideas are indeed the *objects* of the mind when we think or perceive, then realism, certainly direct realism, may be difficult to defend or even articulate.[1]

The quotation from Pasnau occurs in a discussion of Aquinas, how to interpret the role assigned to species: can they be formally (not numerically) identical with external objects, without themselves being the objects we cognize? Species are caused by external processes, hence they may become causal intermediaries. Applied to Locke, does the fact that ideas are caused by physical processes in the environment (and inside the body) make them that which is known? Does the causation of ideas (or with Hume, impressions) by physical objects (Hume's secret powers) prevent direct knowledge of the objects? We might suggest on Locke's behalf that if ideas were signs, that might rule out their being objects of the mind. Ideas in their sign function give us access to their causes, just as words do without the words being what is known. But we have seen that Locke does not develop the few remarks about idea-signs into a doctrine of signs, so this suggestion will probably not apply to him. A related question is, if ideas (or species) are signs, would not they have to arise from a process other than physical? Or perhaps, a physical process that plays a sign role for the perceiver as interpretant?

I

The history of perception theory from Descartes to Kant reveals a move from ontological talk of the *being* of objects in the mind, to the epistemic

---

[1] Analogies or models of the mind are always interesting, sometimes suggestive. Locke talked of dark closets, tablets, engravings. Henry Grove wrote in opposition to Arthur Collier (*Clavis Universalis*, 1713) who had argued against the existence of an external world. (For a discussion of Collier and Grove, see my *Perceptual Acquaintance*, pp. 127–8.) John Deely reminds us of Jacob von Uexküll's "invisible bubble in which alone the environment is rendered meaningful" to each individual (*New Beginnings*, pp. 218–19). Deely's model is of "a kind of geodesic sphere whose interior as well as its surface consists of a series of intersecting lines" (p. 219).

notion of "the being of being known," what I characterized in *Perception and Reality* as an epistemic shift. The philosophers in that period inherited a number of terms, concepts and principles which, in some cases, tied the hands of those who worried about the relation between perceivers and the world. The various suggestions about our knowledge of the external world that we find in those two centuries emerged from within some restrictive boundaries. The language, the vocabulary, writers were forced to employ raised difficulties in the articulation of the views advanced. That language has also often been misread by subsequent readers and interpreters. A brief reminder of some of the changes emerging from the language and concepts used can be helpful as a prelude to a sketch for a realism of appearances.

(a) To know is to *be* the object. Knowing involved acts of the knower and interactions with the objects in the world. The acts acquired their content from the objects. The objects become the contents of the ideas. In Descartes's version, cognitive acts involve ideas as modes of mind; those modes are particularized by the absorption of the object's reality.

(b) Cognition involves signs. This was true for an earlier tradition before Descartes and was reflected in a few passages (e.g., about brain-motion signs) in Descartes.

(c) The language of *being* and the language of substance became less pronounced after Descartes and Arnauld, replaced by the language of ideas. Ideas in some passages in Locke seem to replace objects in our knowledge and awareness, but many passages speak directly of seeing and feeling objects. Berkeley's use of the term "idea" was understood by his contemporaries (and many today) as a move from objects in the world to ideas in the mind. Objects, it was thought, become ideas in Berkeley's account, a view Berkeley vigorously denied.

(d) Hume tried to mediate the tensions between things and ideas, seeking for a way to show that ideas *are* the things, not in the older scholastic tradition of the mind becoming the object, but in some less ontic sense, the sense that our ideas and perceptions are the objects as known.

(e) Kant took Hume farther, giving independence back to ideas or representations.

It is this effort to find a way of recognizing that ideas as contents of awareness are the objects, which marks, I think, the most important feature of these historical developments. Pasnau has shown this same effort at work in the late middle ages. The goal then as with the seventeenth- and eighteenth-century writers is nicely expressed by the quotation from Pasnau at the head of my chapter 6: "Our ideas are, somehow, the objects themselves" (p. 99). Arnauld's insistence that the being of the objects in the mind in Descartes's account was a *cognitive* presence, is one way to reach that goal: ideas capture epistemically the being of objects. Berkeley manifests another sense of this notion, insisting that "existence in the mind" means "is known by the mind." Berkeley rejects ideas as modes of mind, turning them into the things themselves. We might characterize Berkeley's idea-things as Henry Grove's painted globe turned inside out. Hume, of course, echoes that remark by Pasnau: ideas are, at least on the ordinary view, the very things themselves.

If species, ideas or perceptions can be the things themselves, and if we can understand these claims, would we not have some kind of realism? Might it even be a direct realism? I want to explore this possibility, raise some questions, make a few suggestions. I will do so using the term "appearances." That term may seem to imply that there is something that appears to perceivers, so the appearances may not be identical with that which appears. If we consider realism to refer to that which appears, rather than to the appearances themselves, then on the ontology accepted by Descartes, Locke, Hume and perhaps Kant, direct realism is ruled out, as I remarked in chapter 4 with reference to Locke.[2] None of these writers claimed that we perceive that which appears, only what the object itself caused, or helped to cause. Hume did try to defend the ordinary view, but in the end he thought we all do accept a double-existence ontology.

Must a double existence prevent a realism of the appearances? Let's explore this possibility of a realism of appearances, keeping in mind that realism is usually assumed to require the independent existence (independence from the perceiver) of the real.

II

Can appearances meet the independence criterion?

(a) Complete independence
A realism of appearances would be a situation in which we only have the appearances, under the condition of independence. There may be more

---

[2] There cannot, of course, be direct realism of corpuscular structure, since on that theory it is not perceivable. So the only realism of substance could be indirect realism. For that, I suppose, subjective states would have to give us information about (a) the *existence* of substance or (b) of the *properties* of substance. To know that they do so, we would need some argument or inference. In some way, the independent existence of substance would have to be assumed by conjecture or by hypothesis. Perhaps some arguments for the invariance of primary qualities might help the claim. But it would seem difficult to claim *knowledge* of substance from such an argument or hypothesis.

to objects than what appears to us (e.g., corpuscular structure), but if any sense can be made of a realism of appearances, the insensible structure is irrelevant. We might better say that we could have two levels or kinds of realism: a direct realism of appearances and an indirect realism of corpuscular structure, secret springs and principles, real power. For direct realism, the appearances cannot be perceiver-dependent. A *direct realism* of appearances would, I guess, deny the role of the perceiver in how objects appear. They appear to us just as they are *as appearances*. The perceiver plays no role in how objects appear to us to be. Otherwise, we take away the independence of the appearances. So the criterion of independence requires passivity by the perceiver, with respect to how objects appear, to what qualities the appearances have. Does the criterion of independence determine the nature of the perceiver's access to the appearances? What counts as direct access? The answer to this second question is, I think, not very clear. Direct access cannot rule out psychological, mental, cognitive processes of some sort. The need for us to be perceptually aware of the appearances does not itself prevent direct access, whether of appearances or of objects. The way in which that awareness is analyzed or described may determine what counts as direct or indirect access, and hence direct or indirect realism.[3] If, as Locke does on several (but not all) occasions, we characterize perceptual awareness in terms of ideas as "objects" (internal objects), we may be on the road to representationalism, where those idea-objects become intermediaries between perceiver and external objects. If, on the other hand, we characterize ideas or perceptions as the appearances of external objects, the way objects appear to conscious, cognitive perceivers, ideas as intervening entities disappear.

(b) Partial independence

For many seventeenth- and eighteenth-century writers, the appearances are characterized by primary and secondary qualities. The appearances are products of insensible structure *and* the perceiver. How objects appear involves this double dependence relation (causation?). For secondary qualities, the corpuscular structure as well as the perceiver are

---

[3] The notion of *indirect* realism of the appearances may be incoherent. It would claim, I suppose, that we know (perceive) the appearances by means of subjective states. Here, the status of the appearances becomes unclear. Either they are perceiver-independent and hence exist on their own, or they are perceiver-dependent. But the latter is odd. Does this mean that the appearances depend on the subjective states but they are known indirectly? They would have to be dependent on the perceiver without the perceiver being directly aware of them. We would have perceiver-dependence without *esse est percipi* (where "to be perceived" means "I see it, hear it, etc."). But would this not mean that indirect realism of appearances is not possible, that it makes no sense?

involved (dual causality), but for primary qualities, only the corpuscular structure is involved. Descartes and Locke fit here. Primary qualities belong to macro as well as to micro objects. The primary qualities are still independent of the perceiver. But *as experienced*, are they not different from their status as properties of objects? Is this not Berkeley's point, that both kinds of qualities are perceiver-dependent, that is, *just in being perceived*? When any quality is perceived, it as it were changes its status (or locus) from physical quality to mental content, it becomes part of the contents of awareness. So *perceived* qualities differ from qualities as properties of physical objects. To paraphrase Berkeley, what can be like a perceived quality (as appearance) other than a perceived quality? A perceived quality requires a perceiver on whom it is *in part* dependent. That partial dependence need not make the quality a property of the perceiver; the other partner in their causation (the physical object) may pull it back from being just a mental content, an idea as a mode of mind. Recognition of this dual dependence of appearances, on the perceiver and on the external object, may preserve some of the independence required by realism. But the perceiver-dependent part would seem to pull the appearances the other way, towards the perceiver.

Perceiver dependence and realism too

If we follow Berkeley to the extent of saying both kinds of qualities have the same status, so both must be perceiver-dependent, the perceiver independence required for realism seems to be denied, it disappears. Perhaps we might say both kinds of qualities "belong" in some sense to the objects *and* to the perceiver. The nature of the dependence relation differs: the dependence on objects is causal, perceiver-dependence is epistemic. In order for either the primary or secondary qualities to appear, there must be present a cognizing perceiver. The perceiver does not *cause* the qualities to appear, although without a perceiver, there will be no appearances: a noncausal, epistemic-dependence relation. If this suggestion makes sense, perhaps we can say perceiver-dependence does not (need not) make the appearances, the qualities that appear, subjective states of the perceiver. There still can be *appearances*, a *perceiver* and *subjective states* (thoughts, ideas, notions) of the perceiver. Or is it the case that, if x, y and z are caused by w, they are properties of w? On the corpuscular theory accepted by Locke and others, the causal power affecting perceivers is located with the insensible corpuscles. The *perceived* primary qualities are not the qualities of the corpuscles, although the corpuscles have some of those qualities, e.g., hardness, size, motion. The primary qualities we perceive belong to, are ascribed to, the ordinary macro objects in our environment. What the corpuscles cause in perceivers, at least what they partially cause, are not properties of that partial cause. Thus, the causation of ideas or perceived qualities does not determine ownership. Similarly for the other partner in the genesis of perceived qualities: there seems no reason why perceiver-dependence makes what appears properties of the perceiver. So even if appearances require perceivers (they appear to a perceiver), the ontic status of the appearances need not change from properties of macro objects to subjective states. If they are not subjective states, if perceiving them does not change their ontic status, their realism is preserved.

Do appearances have an ontological status?

What can we say, on the terms just described (perceiver-dependence), about the ontic nature of appearances? This seems to be Berkeley's notion of *esse est percipi*. We can remind ourselves of Bradley: the appearances are also real, not just as states of the perceiver, but on their own, even though they are perceiver-dependent. Do we find in Berkeley an attempt to make this point? Three aspects of his account are relevant.

(d1) His denial that ideas are modes of mind; a mode of mind would be a subjective state.

(d2) Existence in the mind = is known by, is perceived.

(d3) His distinction between ideas and notions; the latter would be states of mind.

By the time Berkeley worked on these issues, the language of ideas was in vogue. It was more difficult to treat ideas as distinct from subjective states, hence the need for d3. There were at that time several ways of speaking of ordinary objects *as known*: Descartes's objective reality, Locke's coexisting qualities, Berkeley's ideas that were not modes of mind. Hume's account of the ordinary view in terms of perceptions or objects is a variant on Berkeley's account.

As I suggested in chapter 3, we can speak of a common ontic status for appearances (qualia, phenomena), persons and actions. The three distinctions or couplings – person/man, action/body motion, and appearance/physical object – each refer to a single item, a unit with two aspects or features. The person is not separate from the man, the action is body motion when informed by intention, knowledge and conventions; and the appearances are the objects as known. In each case, something is added to a physical base or object.

The third distinction here is not one between appearances and some insensible reality. The physical objects are ordinary objects, the appearances are the way tables, trees, roses appear to perceivers. The appearances *are* the very things themselves; but I want to retain a distinction between those things as they appear to me and the things that appear (a distinction between ideas and objects?). That is, the appearances are contents of awareness; as contents of awareness they add something to the world over and above the objects themselves. Even if it is the case that those contents match qualities of the object, object qualities are not the same kind of qualities as perceived qualities. Or is it that the contents of awareness cannot, as mental contents, be ascribed to objects? In this way, the perceiver adds something new to the world, just as actions add features not contained in body motion alone. Similarly, the person adds to the man, adds a morally responsible being. But am I forced into saying the physical object does differ from the appearances? Am I not driven to a position of saying objects in themselves are unknown, even though the appearances depend in part upon objects, depend on objects as much as on perceivers (Kant)?

By the phrase, "objects in themselves," I do not mean the insensible corpuscular structure of substances at work in some seventeenth-century writings, but the ordinary objects of trees, stones, roses, desks, etc. To say (or to attempt to say) that the ordinary macro objects are not identical with their appearances to perceivers sounds as if I have introduced another dualism into the account. This is the case, but now we have a dualism of a different sort from that of sensible and insensible. To say objects in themselves are unknown simply means, as Berkeley carefully pointed out, that to think of an object without thinking of it, to perceive it (or know it) without perceiving it is of course impossible, even a manifest contradiction.

Just as Locke's person is the man enhanced by commitment and moral responsibility, so actions are body motions enhanced by intentionality, knowledge, recognition of rules and practices; so ideas, mental contents or appearances are the objects in our world enhanced by being perceived, observed, manipulated, described. Lockean and Kantian perceivers of objects do not inhabit a special world, but instead make the material world more valuable and meaningful. The actions of those perceivers is one of the ways in which value and meaning are added to the world. Appearances, the dual products of objects and perceivers, inhabit a domain between subjective states and unperceived objects. That is the nature of their realism, they have a realist status despite their causal dependence on perceivers and objects.

III

In an important paper, Brigitte Sassen has shown that this is precisely the view Kant took. His empirical objects "are neither representations in us nor objects 'truly' outside or independent of us."[4] Sassen's fascinating presentation of Kant's critics reveals that they badly misunderstood him (the nature of his realism) in much the same way that Berkeley's critics misunderstood Berkeley's realism (I would suggest also, the way Berkeley is usually misunderstood today). The first of many objections against his system Berkeley listed is that he has replaced the world of nature with "a chimerical scheme of ideas . . . All things that exist, exist only in the mind."[5] Sassen indicates that the same charge was made by one of Kant's critics, Feder: "his main complaint is that Kant, like other idealists, reduces everything to representations."[6] That was apparently a common charge against Kant. Sassen's paraphrase of Kant's "Refutation of Idealism" corrects this misunderstanding.

Kant is saying that if I am to make sense of my constantly changing, subjective experience, I must take it as axiomatic that some of the things I am experiencing endure over time when I am not looking at them. Otherwise, there would be nothing that could serve as a landmark or a clock and no way, therefore, to even begin making sense of my experience. So I am necessarily constrained to infer objects that are "behind" what I experience, not as things in themselves – nor, however, as mere representations in me.[7]

She agrees that Kant's language does tend to mislead and confuse his readers, his "references to 'things outside of me', to 'the existence of actual things', to 'outer sense' and to the 'immediate consciousness of the existence of other things outside me' and might suggest that he does want to take the realist turn his contemporaries demanded," a realm of things in themselves (p. 444).

John McDowell (in *Mind and World*) endorses and reformulates much of Kant's analysis. McDowell's book is an important contribution to one of the central issues in modern philosophy: the relation between perceivers and the world. His text is Kant's dictum, "Thoughts without content are empty, intuitions without concepts are blind."[8] McDowell also uses Kant's combination of spontaneity of the understanding and receptivity, passivity, of the sensibility. McDowell rejects two features of Kant's account of these two functions. (1) Kant's reference to receptivity as "the

---

[4] "Critical Idealism in the Eyes of Kant's Contemporaries," *Journal of the History of Philosophy* 35 (July 1997), 446. [5] Berkeley, *Principles*, §34. [6] Sassen, "Critical Idealism," pp. 425–6.
[7] *Ibid.*, pp. 441–2. [8] Kant, *Critique of Pure Reason*, B75.

mode in which we are affected by objects."[9] (2) Kant's assertion that representations as intuitions are in "immediate relation to an object" and
"no concept is ever related to an object immediately."[10] McDowell reads
the affection relation as involving a transcendental or insensible realm,
as I believe it does.[11] I have a few comments later on McDowell's reluctance to accept any such realm into his own view of knowledge and
reality.

Of more importance for the statement of McDowell's own view is his
uneasiness with the immediate-mediate distinction. The term "immediate" runs throughout philosophical discussions of perception from the
seventeenth century to the twentieth. Locke spoke of ideas as the immediate objects of the mind when it thinks (not when it perceives). Berkeley
of course also employs that term. Many twentieth-century philosophers
have made appeals to "the Given" as supplying the basic sensory mate-
rials on which cognition works. McDowell writes against this notion; it
rests, he believes, on the mistaken notion that there are "non-conceptual
impacts from outside the realm of thought" (p. 7). It is as if the appeals
to such a basic datum assume an outer boundary to our thoughts, such
a datum being "an alien force, the causal impact of the world, operating
outside the control of our spontaneity" (p. 8). McDowell insists that there
can be no "extra conceptual impact on sensibility" (p. 14). He seems to
allow that the world does make impressions on our senses but those
impressions "are already possessed of conceptual content" (p. 18; cf. pp.
23, 39). Just what the world is for him is not all that clear. He admits that
there are "constraints" on our spontaneity, on our thinking, "but not
from outside what is *thinkable*" (p. 28; cf. p. 41).[12] McDowell warns that we
must be careful in our talk of "impingements" on our senses.

This talk of impingements on our senses is not an invitation to suppose that the
whole dynamic system, the medium within which we think, is held in place by
extra-conceptual links to something outside it. That is just to stress again that
we must not picture an outer boundary around the sphere of the conceptual,
with a reality outside the boundary impinging inward on the system. (p. 34)

Such a notion of something affecting our senses from beyond the limits
of our thought opens the way for a causal relation between the world

[9] *Ibid.*, B75; cf. B93.   [10] *Ibid.*, B93.
[11] For a discussion of that relation, see my *Perception and Reality* (pp. 175–8), and Moltke Gram, *The
Transcendental Turn*.
[12] Compare with Berkeley, *Principles*, Section 3: "For as to what is said of the absolute existence of
unthinking things without any relation to their being perceived, that seems perfectly unintelligible."

and perceivers. "Any impingements across such an outer boundary could only be causal, and not rational" (p. 34). McDowell's way of expressing the point made by the writers discussed in chapter 2, and the suggestion by Descartes – that there is a noncausal, meaning relation between the world and perceivers – is to say that "in experience the world exerts a rational influence on our thinking" (*ibid.*, cf. p. 68).[13] His rational relations play, I think, the role of those noncausal, semantic relations I have argued for. He asserts emphatically that "We need to bring responsiveness to meaning back into the operations of our natural sentient capacities as such, even while we insist that responsiveness to meaning cannot be captured in naturalistic terms, so long as 'naturalistic' is glossed in terms of the realm of law" (p. 77).[14]

McDowell contrasts the realm of law (nature) with the realm of reason (meaning, justification), but he urges us to redefine "nature" in such a way that it comes within the realm of reason and conceptualization. He seems to want a naturalism "that makes room for meaning" (p. 75), although he admits that naturalizing meaning might not really provide a proper naturalism. We see the same struggle in McDowell as is found in Kant: to find a way to naturalize our cognitive processes, to make some of them the result of an independent reality, an empirical not a transcendental reality. The trick, at least for McDowell, is how to maintain that conceptualization is present in the very impressions that owe in some way their existence if not their function to the empirical world. For Kant, the empirical world is the product of the combination of the activity of the understanding (spontaneity) and the receptivity of the senses. Kant boot-straps sensibility with the affection relation, an action from a nonempirical world. This is just the move that McDowell wants to avoid. Whether the nonempirical world in Kant's account is in fact another world, or whether it is just the world in which we live but prior to our being aware of objects, is a question of some debate. McDowell recognizes that if he is to avoid an idealism where the

---

[13] McDowell characterizes Donald Davidson, against whom he writes, as saying "a causal, not rational, linkage between thinking and independent reality will do" (p. 68).

[14] Although McDowell mentions "perceptual experience" in several places (pp. xxiii, 26, 85, 89), he does not pretend to offer a theory of perception. He employs locutions such as being "open to the way things manifestly are" (p. xx); "What perceptually appears to a subject that things are thus and so" (p. xviii); "In experience one takes in, for instance sees, *that things are thus and so*" (p. 9; cf. p. 25); in veridical experience "that things are thus and so . . . are aspects of the layout of the world: it is how things are" (p. 26). None of these phrases is accompanied with an account of how things come to appear thus and so. To fill in the details of the perceptual process is not part of McDowell's program. Nor is there any mention of the role of neurophysiology in our perceptual experience.

spontaneity of the understanding is the only determining factor in the formation and discovery of objects, he must find in receptivity some contribution other than what the understanding brings to experience, some "constraints" upon our conceptualization. But he insists that there is no reality "located outside the boundary that encloses the conceptual sphere" (p. 41). If the contributions of sensibility are already conceptualized, does that not threaten to dilute any contribution from the senses? He wants to have only the empirical world while having independence too. He puts the crucial question to himself: "But how can the empirical world be genuinely independent of us, if we are partly responsible for its fundamental structure?" (p. 42). Concepts are at work in all levels of experience, but they function at the level of sense experience, in spite of our being "acted on by independent reality" (p. 67). McDowell is very close to Kant when he uses Kant's phrase, "outer experience," and claims that an independent reality makes impressions on us, impressions which have conceptual content.[15] Kant employs the notion of affection, McDowell speaks of "constraints." The nature of the source of affection and the constraint remains for both authors somewhat obscure. Neither wants us to think of the "ordinary empirical world" as if it is "constituted by appearances of a reality beyond" our experience (p. 98).

A realism of appearances may not require that appearances are *of* another world, a distinction between appearances and that which appears. Perhaps a phenomenalism might succeed in finding features in experience that are not under our control. Kant can be read this way: outer representations exhibit an order and sequence that we cannot control. Berkeley's realism, I have argued, recognizes that there is a uniformity and lawfulness of observable and predictable phenomena. For Berkeley, there seems to be no reality behind or beyond the reality of perceived objects. For a realism of appearances combined with some notion of a reality as more than the appearances, the problem is how to talk about or refer to those other aspects of reality, the real causes and powers (Hume), the source of affection (Kant). When our language for talking about the world is restricted to experiential words, to words, phrases and concepts that describe features of an observable world, references to nonexperiential components (causes, forces, powers) are faced with indirectness and vagueness. We may simply have to accept the fact that there are aspects of a philosopher's system, especially the ontology,

---

[15] There is a similarity here with Descartes's ideas which as modes of mind strictly lack content, the content being added by objects: objects particularize the ideas.

that cannot be encompassed within the epistemology advanced by, or even the conditions for intelligibility accepted by, its author. Many will find such a suggestion quite unsatisfactory, but the alternative may be equally unacceptable: to translate what seems to be references to nonempirical claims into experiential terms. Some of our most honored philosophers may believe more than they can say.

Bibliography

Ackerman, Diane. *Natural History of the Senses*. New York: Random House, 1990.

Arnauld, Antoine. *Des vrayes et des fausses idées, contre ce qu'enseigne l'auteur de la Recherche de la verité*. Cologne: N. Schouten, 1683.

   On True and False Ideas. Trans. with an introductory essay by Stephen Gaukroger. Manchester: Manchester University Press, 1990.

Berkeley, George. *Works*. Ed. A. A. Luce and T. E. Jessop. 9 vols. London: Nelson, 1948–57.

Bracken, Harry M. *Berkeley*. London: Macmillan, 1974.

Bradley, F. H. *Appearance and Reality: A Metaphysical Essay*. London: G. Allen & Unwin, 1893.

Broadie, Alexander. *Notion and Object: Aspects of Late Medieval Epistemology*. Oxford: Clarendon Press, 1989.

Chalmers, David J. *The Conscious Mind: In Search of a Fundamental Theory*. Oxford: Oxford University Press, 1996.

Churchland, Paul M. *The Engine of Reason, the Seat of the Soul: A Philosophical Journey into the Brain*. Cambridge, Mass.: MIT Press, 1995.

Collier, Arthur. *Clavis Universalis, or A New Inquiry after Truth; Being a Demonstration of the Non-Existence or Impossibility of an External World*. London: R. Gosling, 1713.

Coulter, Jeff. "Neural Cartesianism. Comments on the Epistemology of the Cognitive Sciences," in *The Future of the Cognitive Revolution*, ed. Johnson and Erneling, pp. 293–301.

Crane, Tim (ed.) *The Contents of Experience*. Cambridge: Cambridge University Press, 1992.

Cummins, Phillip D. and Günter Zöller (eds.) *Minds, Ideas and Objects: Essays on the Theory of Representation in Modern Philosophy*. North American Kant Society Studies in Philosophy, vol. 2. Atascadero, Calif.: Ridgeview, 1992.

Deely, John. *New Beginnings: Early Modern Philosophy and Postmodern Thought*. Toronto: University of Toronto Press, 1994.

Descartes, René. *Oeuvres de Descartes*. Ed. Ch. Adam and P. Tannery. 12 vols. Paris: L. Cerf, 1897–1910.

   The Philosophical Writings of Descartes. Trans. J. Cottingham, R. Stoothoff and D. Murdoch. 3 vols. Cambridge: Cambridge University Press, 1984–91.

   Treatise of Man. French text with translation and commentary by Thomas Steele Hall. Cambridge, Mass.: Harvard University Press, 1972.

Oeuvres philosophiques. Ed. F. Alquié. 3 vols. Paris: Garnier Frères, 1963–73.

Flage, Daniel E. *Berkeley's Doctrine of Notions: A Reconstruction Based on His Theory of Meaning*. London: Croom Helm, 1987.

"Relative Ideas and Notions," in *Minds, Ideas and Objects*, ed. Cummins and Zöller, pp. 235–53.

Foster, John and Howard Robinson (eds.) *Essays on Berkeley: A Tercentennial Celebration*. Oxford: Clarendon Press, 1985.

Garrett, Don. *Cognition and Commitment in Hume's Philosophy*. New York: Oxford University Press, 1997.

Gillet, Grant. *Representation, Meaning and Thought*. Oxford: Clarendon Press, 1992.

Gram, Moltke S. *The Transcendental Turn: The Foundation of Kant's Idealism*. Gainesville: University of Florida Press, 1984.

Grove, Henry. *An Essay Towards a Demonstration of the Soul's Immateriality*. London: Printed for J. Clark, 1718.

Hardin, Clyde. *Color for Philosophers: Unweaving the Rainbow*. Expanded edn. Indianapolis: Hackett, 1988.

Hume, David. *Essays Moral, Political and Literary*. Ed. Eugene Miller. Rev. edn. Indianapolis: Liberty Fund, 1985.

Hume's Philosophical Works. Ed. T. H. Green and T. H. Grose. 4 vols. London, 1874–5.

Enquiries concerning Human Understanding and concerning the Principles of Morals. Ed. L. A. Selby-Bigge. 3rd edn., revised by P. H. Nidditch. Oxford: Clarendon Press, 1975. Most of my references are to the *Enquiry concerning Human Understanding*; I cite this in the text by the word *Enquiry*.

A Treatise of Human Nature. Ed. L. A. Selby-Bigge. 2nd edn., revised by P. H. Nidditch. Oxford: Clarendon Press, 1978. This edition contains *An Abstract of a Book Lately Published. . . .*, pp. 642–62.

Jackson, Frank. "Mental Causation." *Mind* 105, no. 419 (1996), 377–413.

Johnson, David Martel and Christina E. Erneling (eds.) *The Future of the Cognitive Revolution*. New York: Oxford University Press, 1997.

Kant, Immanuel. *Critique of Pure Reason*. Trans. N. K. Smith. London: Macmillan, 1950.

Lloyd, A. C. "The Self in Berkeley's Philosophy," in *Essays on Berkeley: A Tercentennial Celebration*, ed. Foster and Robinson.

Locke, John. *Mr. Locke's Reply to The Right Reverend the Lord Bishop of Worchester's Answer to his Second Letter* (1695). In *Works* (1823), vol. 4, pp. 192–498.

Drafts for the Essay concerning Human Understanding, and Other Philosophical Writings. Ed. Peter H. Nidditch and G. A. J. Rogers. Vol. 1. Oxford: Clarendon Press, 1990.

An Essay concerning Human Understanding. Ed. Peter H. Nidditch. Oxford: Clarendon Press, 1975.

Some Thoughts concerning Education. Ed. John W. and Jean S. Yolton. Oxford: Clarendon Press, 1989.

Lowe, E. J. *Locke on Human Understanding*. London: Routledge, 1995.

"Experience and its Objects," in *The Contents of Experience*, ed. Tim Crane, pp. 79–104.

"Perception: A Causal Representative Theory," in *New Representationalisms*, ed. Edmond Wright, pp. 136–52.

Subjects of Experience. Cambridge: Cambridge University Press, 1996.

McDowell, John. *Mind and World.* Cambridge, Mass.: Harvard University Press, 1996.

Malebranche, Nicolas. *Oeuvres complètes.* Direction: André Robinet. 20 vols. Paris: J. Vrin, 1958–70.

Mayne, Charles. *An Essay concerning Rational Notions.* London: W. Innys, 1733.

Mayne, Zachary. *Two Dissertations concerning Sense and the Imagination; with an Essay on Consciousness.* London: J. Tonson, 1728.

Oakes, Robert. "Representational Sensing: What's the Problem," in *New Representationalisms*, ed. Edmond Wright, pp. 70–87.

Pasnau, Robert. *Theories of Cognition in the Later Middle Ages.* Cambridge: Cambridge University Press, 1997.

Priestley, Joseph. *Disquisitions Relating to Matter and Spirit; To Which Is Added, The History of the Philosophical Doctrine concerning the Origin of the Soul, and the Nature of Matter.* 2 vols. London: J. Johnson, 1777.

Robinson, Howard. "Physicalism, Externalism and Perceptual Representation," in *New Representationalisms*, ed. Edmond Wright, pp. 103–14.

Sassen, Brigitte. "Critical Idealism in the Eyes of Kant's Contemporaries," *Journal of the History of Philosophy* 35 (1997), 421–55.

Savellos, Elias E. and Ünit D. Yalçin (eds.) *Supervenience: New Essays.* Cambridge: Cambridge University Press, 1995.

Siewert, Charles P. *The Significance of Consciousness.* Princeton: Princeton University Press, 1998.

Strawson, Galen. *The Secret Connexion: Causation, Realism and David Hume.* Oxford: Clarendon Press, 1989.

Sutton, John. *Philosophy and Memory Traces: Descartes to Connectionism.* Cambridge: Cambridge University Press, 1998.

Tomida, Yasuhiko. *Idea and Thing: The Deep Structure of Locke's Theory of Knowledge.* Dordrecht: Kluwer, 1995. Reprinted from *Analecta Husserliana*, 46 (1995), 3–143.

Winkler, Kenneth P. "The New Hume." *The Philosophical Review*, 100, no. 4 (October 1991), 541–79.

Berkeley: An Interpretation. Oxford: Clarendon Press, 1989.

Wright, Edmond (ed.) *New Representationalisms: Essays in the Philosophy of Perception.* Avebury Series in Philosophy. Aldershot: Avebury, 1993.

Wright, John P. *The Sceptical Realism of David Hume.* Manchester: Manchester University Press, 1983.

Yolton, John W. *Locke and the Compass of Human Understanding.* Cambridge: Cambridge University Press, 1990

Locke and French Materialism. Oxford: Clarendon Press, 1991.

A Locke Dictionary. Oxford: Blackwell, 1993.

Perceptual Acquaintance from Descartes to Reid. Minneapolis: University of Minnesota Press; Oxford: Blackwell, 1984.

Thinking Matter: Materialism in Eighteenth-Century Britain. Minneapolis: University of Minnesota Press; Oxford: Blackwell, 1983.
"Schoolmen, Logic and Philosophy," in *The History of the University of Oxford*, vol. 5, ed. L. S. Sutherland and L. G. Mitchell (Oxford: Clarendon Press, 1986), ch. 20, pp. 565–91.
Perception and Reality: A History from Descartes to Kant. Ithaca: Cornell University Press, 1996.

Index